Mango Millionaire

Radhika Gupta is one of the most dynamic and inspiring voices in India's financial services industry today. As the Managing Director & CEO of Edelweiss Mutual Fund, she has redefined leadership in asset management with a vision rooted in innovation, inclusivity and impact. A global citizen with deep Indian roots, Radhika worked in a wide range of organizations such as Microsoft, McKinsey & Company and AQR Capital, before co-founding Forefront Capital Management, later acquired by Edelweiss Financial Services in 2014. At just thirty-four, she took charge as CEO of Edelweiss Mutual Fund, becoming one of the youngest leaders in the industry.

A prominent board member and former Vice Chairperson of the Association of Mutual Funds in India (AMFI), Radhika is also widely recognized for her contributions to investor awareness and financial literacy. Her authentic communication style – epitomized by her viral TEDx talk 'The Girl with a Broken Neck' – has made her a relatable role model for young professionals and women in leadership across the country. In 2023, she became a household name after her appearance on *Shark Tank India* Season 3, where her investor acumen and entrepreneurial passion attracted the attention of a much wider audience.

An alumnus of the prestigious Jerome Fisher Program in Management and Technology at the University of Pennsylvania, Radhika graduated with dual degrees in Computer Science (Engineering) and Economics (Finance and Management). Beyond boardrooms and screens, she is an advocate for self-growth and resilience. Her bestselling book *Limitless* (2022) reflects her personal journey of overcoming challenges and unlocking her potential – values that shine through in *Mango Millionaire* as well, geared towards helping readers take charge of their financial destinies with clarity and courage.

Her remarkable contributions have been widely recognized through numerous awards and honours, including: *Fortune India* 50 Most Powerful Women in Business (2020), *Economic Times* 40 Under 40 Business Leaders Award (2021), Young Global Leader by the World Economic Forum (2022), *Business Today* Most Powerful Women in Indian Business (2019, 2021, 2022, 2023 and 2024), *Forbes* W Power Self-made Women Award (2022), *GQ* Most Influential 30 young Indians (2023).

With over two decades of rich experience in the financial services industry, Niranjan Avasthi is a seasoned leader known for his deep insights on mutual funds, investor behaviour and market trends. Since 2017, he has been spearheading key strategic initiatives across products, marketing and digital functions at Edelweiss Mutual Fund, where he currently serves as Senior Vice President.

A Cost and Management Accountant (ICAI) and MCom graduate, Niranjan is also a rank-holder in PGDMM from Pune University. His academic rigour is matched by his practical wisdom, making him a trusted voice in the Indian personal finance landscape. He is frequently featured by leading financial publications like *The Economic Times*, *Mint* and others, and is a familiar face on business news channels such as *CNBC TV18*, *ET Now* and *Zee Business*, where he simplifies complex market developments for everyday investors. In *Mango Millionaire*, Niranjan brings his wealth of knowledge to help readers build practical financial habits, demystify mutual funds, and take confident steps toward wealth creation.

Mango Millionaire

SMART MONEY MANAGEMENT FOR A SWEETER LIFE

RADHIKA GUPTA
WITH NIRANJAN AVASTHI

MACMILLAN BUSINESS

First published 2025 by Macmillan Business
an imprint of Pan Macmillan Publishing India Private Limited
707 Kailash Building
26 K. G. Marg, New Delhi 110001
www.panmacmillan.co.in

Pan Macmillan, The Smithson, 6 Briset Street, Farringdon, London EC1M 5NR
Associated companies throughout the world
www.panmacmillan.com

ISBN 978-93-6113-216-2

Copyright © Radhika Gupta and Niranjan Avasthi, 2025

The moral rights of the author have been asserted.

The views expressed in this book are the authors' own and the facts reported by them have been verified by the publisher to the extent possible. The publisher hereby disclaims any liability to any party for loss, damages or disruptions caused by the same.

All rights reserved. No part of this publication may be reproduced, stored in or introduced into a retrieval system, or transmitted, in any form, or by any means (electronic, mechanical, photocopying, recording or otherwise) without the prior written permission of the publisher. Any person who does any unauthorized act in relation to this publication may be liable to criminal prosecution and civil claims for damages.

5 7 9 8 6 4

This book is sold subject to the condition that it shall not, by way of trade or otherwise, be lent, re-sold, hired out, or otherwise circulated without the publisher's prior consent in any form of binding or cover other than that in which it is published and without a similar condition including this condition being imposed on the subsequent purchaser.

Typeset in Sabon LT Std by R. Ajith Kumar, New Delhi
Printed and bound in India by Replika Press Pvt. Ltd.

To all the Indians who choose dal chawal over avocado toast, this book is for you

'Money doesn't buy happiness, but it pays for the ingredients.'

– A mango millionaire's wisdom

CONTENTS

Introduction: Money Is Confusing.   1
We Tried to Fix That.

PART I: THE FUNDAMENTALS   9

1. Your Relationship with Money: Love, Hate or It's Complicated?   11
2. Money 101: It's Part of Life's Syllabus   23
3. Savings Versus Investing: Fuelling Up to Hit the Road   35
4. Debt: A Friend in Need, a Foe in Greed   51
5. Risk: Don't Buy a Ticket to the Wrong Ride   62
6. Returns: Good Enough Is Actually Great   71
7. Taxes: From CTC to Reality, Mind the Gap   82
8. Insurance: The Parachute, Not the Plane   95

PART II: THE BUILDING BLOCKS   107

9. Real Estate: Buy a Home, Not the Hype   109
10. Gold: From Trousseau to Treasury   120
11. Fixed Income: A Sensible Sidekick   128
12. Equities: Owning Tata without the Tension   142

Part III: Making Money Work For You — 153

13. Mutual Funds I: Welcome to the Financial Food Court — 155
14. Mutual Funds II: Maruti or Mercedes – What's Your Ride? — 169
15. Portfolio Building: Lessons from The Great Indian Thali — 188
16. Financial Tools and Features: The SIP Family — 199
17. Money Hygiene: Clean Up to Cash In — 210
18. Money Behaviour: Don't Follow the Herd, Lead the Pack — 220
19. Financial Advice: Because Google Isn't Enough — 230
20. The Economy and Money: The Kite and the Wind — 241
21. Money and Family: Little Lessons to Big Legacies — 250

Afterword: The End and the Beginning — 259
Acknowledgements — 262

INTRODUCTION

Money Is Confusing. We Tried to Fix That.

A few months ago, I was at Dr Babasaheb Ambedkar International Airport, Nagpur, rushing through security, juggling my laptop, boarding pass and handbag, when I noticed that the man behind me in the queue was watching me, waiting to say something. I nodded at him, encouraging him to speak.

'Madam, *aap mutual funds mein ho?* (do you work in mutual funds?)' he asked.

I nodded. He probably followed me on social media or recognized me from TV when I was on *Shark Tank India* Season 3, doling out financial advice.

'Returns haven't been great for the last three months,' he said, lowering his voice like we were discussing a state secret. 'What do you think I should do?'

Before I could respond, another passenger, fumbling with his belt, chimed in: 'Yes, tell us! Is this a good time to buy Bank Nifty?'

And just like that, I found myself in the middle of an impromptu stock market seminar at 6 AM at airport security. Oh, the life of a mutual fund professional! I could be at a wedding, a doctor's appointment or shopping for sarees – the moment people find out who I am, it is a done thing that they'll ask me for a stock tip.

Take my cousin's wedding for example. The venue was aglow with fairy lights, the DJ was blasting 'London *Thumakda*' and I was peacefully enjoying my paneer tikka, grateful for the only true reason people attend weddings: the food. Suddenly, a long-lost uncle materialized beside me, grinning like he had just discovered the stock market's biggest secret. '*Beta* I'm wondering if I should start an SIP or invest lump sum …'

Scooping an extra gulab jamun onto his plate, he explained, 'someone in my office says the market is going to crash so mutual funds are risky.'

I smiled. 'Then why are you asking me, uncle?'

He grinned sheepishly. 'Just confirming!'

You see what I mean? Everyone wants financial tips, but usually, it's all they want. It is rare that people can verbalize the desire to truly learn about money, even though that is what is really at the core of their questions. These random interactions and conversations are what drove me to write this book. To help people understand that money management is personal. And confusing. And emotional. And despite all the stock market apps, YouTube videos and WhatsApp university forwards, people still don't know what to do with it.

As mutual fund professionals, Niranjan Avasthi, my

colleague and the co-author of this book, and I have been asked financial questions that range from brilliant to utterly confused. They come from working professionals, rich businessmen, bureaucrats, housewives – everyone! Each question has a story behind it. Some come from the joy of triumph, others from the disenchantment of failure, but all of them open the gates to invaluable lessons.

One story comes to mind: Mridula, who has come to feel more like family than a friend to me over the years, lived a picture-perfect life. Married to a top executive, she had access to every luxury – a high-rise apartment in Mumbai, fancy cars and lavish vacations. But perfection often has a way of unravelling in unexpected ways.

One evening, her husband complained of chest pain. What appeared minor at first escalated rapidly, and gripped with panic, she dialled for an ambulance. At the hospital, the medical staff's urgency in attending to her husband only heightened her dread. When she saw the doctor finally approaching, his face told her everything. Her husband was gone. He had been taken by a massive heart attack without warning.

Mridula's world crumbled overnight. The man who had been her rock so far was suddenly no more. She'd often feel overwhelmed by grief, yet it was not the only storm she faced. Financial matters had always been her husband's arena, and now here she was, drowning in a sea of unfamiliar paperwork. Bank statements, insurance papers and investment records – things she had barely ever glanced at, earlier – all blurred into a confusing mix of numbers and jargon. She didn't know where to even begin. She had no idea how much her husband had left behind, or how to manage the funds in her own account. Her mind spiralled into anxiety: *What if there's not enough money? What will happen to my children? How will I manage?*

Her worries were soon alleviated, however, after financially aware friends and family, including myself, did a systematic analysis of the couple's accounts to find that her husband had left behind a sizeable corpus. There were assets of various kinds: mutual funds, fixed deposits (FD), real estate and insurance policies. Relief washed over her, but she felt a pang of guilt – she had all this wealth and not the slightest clue how to use or deploy it. She had simply never had to learn until crisis came knocking at her door.

Niranjan too has his own set of similar stories to share. One particularly memorable instance involves one of his middle-aged cousins, Rohit, a man constantly on the lookout for the next big investment opportunity. Cryptocurrency had recently caught his attention. This was during a period when social media was teeming with success stories of overnight millionaires who claimed to have struck gold from investing in crypto. As Rohit watched influencers and his peers brag about their crypto gains, his fascination grew into an obsession. He too wanted a piece of the pie. Despite Niranjan repeatedly advising him to tread carefully, he couldn't resist.

'The crypto market is highly volatile,' Niranjan would tell him. But promises of high returns and the fear of missing out proved far more compelling. Swept up in the frenzy, Rohit decided to put a significant portion of his savings into a particularly new, hyped-up digital coin. The buzz around it was that investments would be doubled in less than a month's time.

When I heard about this, in my movie buff brain, I could almost hear the actor Akshay Kumar's character in *Phir Hera Pheri* (2006), a scam artist, peddling his chit-fund scheme with the (false) promise of '*pachhees din mein paisa* double! (double your money in twenty-five days!)' At first, Rohit's decision seemed brilliant. The value of the coin shot up and so did his confidence. He ignored Niranjan's persistent reminders to diversify his investments and secure his gains. Then, the inevitable happened. The developers of the cryptocurrency executed a 'rug pull' – a scam where they abruptly withdrew all funds, leaving investors with worthless tokens. Rohit's investment evaporated overnight, and with it, his dreams of quick riches. Niranjan's words echoed in his mind then, but it was too late to recover what he had lost. He had to learn his lesson the hard way, unfortunately.

The thing is that people like Mridula and Rohit are not alone. Most people struggle with money because they don't know how to make it work for them. Life, for most of us, is already a grind. Long working weeks (sometimes even seventy hours a week!), endless and tiring commutes, rising inflation, puny salaries, high-interest loans ... personal finance just feels like an additional chore. We think it's too complicated anyway.

The fact remains, however, that Indians are amongst the hardest workers in the world. And if we play our cards right, our money can work even harder than us to get us the life we dream of.

Why This Book

So why do people avoid personal finance like the plague? We figured it is because it is often shrouded in complexity and jargon. The sheer volume of information can feel really scary. Our goal is to simplify this into easy-to-understand ideas and open up the world of money for you.

While numerous books have been written on topics like value investing or stock market strategies, very few of them are tailored to the needs of the average Indian investor. India's money game is entirely different from the rest of the world. What works on Wall Street won't always fly in Borivali, Vasant Kunj or Jayanagar. Our financial landscape has its own twists and turns, risks and opportunities. You need advice in your own language, not some global strategy that doesn't factor in how *you* spend and invest.

Moreover, personal finance is not taught in our schools, sadly. Most people learn by trial and error, often at the cost of their savings, and that just doesn't feel fair. So here's our book: Simple, friendly and proudly *desi*.

Since the onset of the COVID-19 pandemic, many people have started investing by opening demat accounts, buying shares and starting SIPs with just a few taps on their smartphones. But the ease of investing hasn't necessarily translated to better financial decisions or outcomes. This book is here to help fill that gap between knowledge and accessibility.

What This Book Is (and Isn't)

This isn't a stock tip hotline or a get-rich-quick manual. It's also not some jargon-heavy textbook that will just collect dust on your bookshelf. Think of it as a smart, no-nonsense guide in personal finance you can actually read, use and return to whenever you need to. We've tried to break down key concepts and supplemented our explanations with real-world stories of people just like you so you can feel competent and confident to start investing. While you are welcome to read the book in bits and pieces and focus on the chapters and ideas that matter most to you, we have divided it into three parts. The first talks about foundational concepts of money like savings versus investing, risk and returns. The second delves into the key asset classes, the building blocks of an investment portfolio – equity, gold, debt, etc. – and aims to help you build an in-depth understanding of each of them. The third ties it all together, sharing the best of our wisdom to help you make your money work to meet your goals and your needs.

Both Niranjan and I are movie lovers, so there are plenty of references to Bollywood films peppered throughout the book. A scene from *Love Aaj Kal* (2009) comes to mind: towards the end of the film, Saif Ali Khan's character tells Deepika Padukone that Romeo–Juliet, Heer–Ranjha, Laila–Majnu exist only in stories. *Aam janta* – the 'mango people' – don't aspire to such legendary feats; they simply want to live a good life with the person they love.

Well, what is true for love is also true for money. Not everybody aspires to becoming a legendary investor – most people just want to live a comfortable life where the money they earn feels enough for them.

So dear 'mango person', are you ready to become a 'mango millionaire'?

Let's get started!

PART I

THE FUNDAMENTALS

1

YOUR RELATIONSHIP WITH MONEY

Love, Hate or It's Complicated?

An Unusual Cup of Coffee

Imagine this: You're chilling in a super cosy café. The smell of fresh espresso in the air mixes perfectly with the scent of freshly baked pastries. Soft music is playing in the background and you're dressed in your favourite outfit. But here's the twist – you're on a date with *Money*.

You are totally absorbed in conversation, eagerly asking Money all the questions you have always wanted to: 'What makes you happy? What frustrates you? What is your story? What are your dreams?' To your surprise, Money is willingly spilling the tea while drinking their coffee. They talk about how much they love it when you appreciate them – like that time you saved up for that dream vacation, or made a killer investment. But they also share their grievances, like the time you splurged on stuff you did not even need, or the time they felt ghosted because you ignored your finances.

The conversation is on fire and you are all ears. But what if you weren't? What if, instead of paying attention, you kept zoning out or kept giving them the classic '*aur batao* (tell me more)' every few minutes, like nothing they were saying was interesting to you?

Money would certainly feel like you were simply not interested in them. The date would be a flop, wouldn't it? Ignoring your finances is like yawning when your date is telling you an interesting story about their lives. It is never going to end well. But when you are fully locked in and willing to engage, you can set about building a relationship that can help you live your best life. So the next time you're metaphorically on a date with Money, make sure you're really tuned in, because just like any relationship, if you don't give money the effort and attention it deserves, it will get messy. One of my friends learned this the hard way.

A Journey with Money

One day, while I was brainstorming for a project at my office, my phone buzzed. I glanced at the screen and saw it was Ajay, a buddy I hadn't heard from in forever. I picked up, thinking it would just be for a casual catch-up, but no – he was in a financial pickle and needed advice.

Back in the days, Ajay had always been *the* guy. He'd get dropped to school in a Maruti Esteem. While most people argued with rickshaw drivers or clung onto buses for dear life, Esteem owners pulled up with their sunglasses on like movie stars. Esteem was the car of the season – and only one of the many expensive cars in his family's fleet.

He grew up to fancy imported watches and fine dining at expensive restaurants. In the Delhi of the '90s, going to Berco's was quite a flex. Their chilli chicken and hot and sour soup were an unparalleled luxury. If you were invited there for a school friend's birthday, you knew that friend was *really* rich. It was where Ajay threw all his birthday parties.

But he was always looking for more. He had the Esteem, but then he wanted the Lancer. Got the Lancer, but then he started eyeing something even flashier. His wishlist was never-ending. Fast forward to now – the guy who once had everything was strapped for cash. The irony? Other friends, who came from much more modest backgrounds, were standing on solid financial ground.

Even though I couldn't possibly help him out of his financial struggles over a phone call, Ajay's story got me thinking about how our money habits are shaped by what we see around us while growing up. My parents always told me, 'Don't chase things you can't afford until you *can* afford them.' They weren't trying to kill my vibe – they just wanted to keep me from falling into the trap of wanting more than I could handle, which inevitably ends in debt.

Honestly, I am pretty glad I listened. It is a lesson rooted in the Indian middle-class ethos of '*sasta, sundar, tikau* (cheap, good-looking, durable)' or SST. SST happens to be my mother's favourite acronym. Her other favourite is VFM (Value for Money).

From VFM to YOLO

When I was a kid, my parents would always buy me clothes a size too big. 'You'll grow into it,' they would say. This is a life hack I continue to follow to this day, alongside, of course, the tenet of everything having to be VFM. VFM was the unofficial motto of the Indian middle class for Gen X and Gen Y. It was a way of life, whether it was picking schools for children, buying a house or even getting a new sofa. The goal was always the same: maximize value, minimize waste and ensure everything could survive a mini apocalypse.

But this mindset was not born in a vacuum. It was shaped by the realities of India before the liberalization of the '90s. The government had an iron grip on everything and starting a business was like trying to solve a Rubik's Cube blindfolded – licenses for this, permits for that. Even for owning a scooter one needed to endure mountains of paperwork. It was an era that has since come to be known as the License Raj. Entrepreneurship was a distant dream for most and consumer choice was as limited as the choice of entertainment on TV. All we had back then were the black-and-white Doordarshan channels.

Even pop culture mirrored this reality. Think of the iconic 'angry young man' of the 1970s. Immortalized by the writer duo Salim–Javed's films like *Zanjeer* (1973), and *Deewaar* (1975), this hero was angry, frustrated and always ready to fight the system. He did not sing and dance around trees. He did not crack jokes. All he did was brood and fight and rage against a system where red tape muffled aspiration.

Then came the '90s. A severe balance of payments crisis prompted then Finance Minister Dr Manmohan Singh, under the leadership of Prime Minister P. V. Narasimha Rao, to introduce radical reforms. Overnight, the country went from a closed, license-driven economy to a liberalized one. Import tariffs? Slashed. Markets? Deregulated. Foreign investment? Come on in!

Suddenly, India was on the fast track to becoming one of the fastest-growing economies of the world. This economic glow-up led to the formation of a more affluent society. Gen Z and Gen Alpha were born in this new India and grew up in a blingy YOLO (You Only Live Once) world. Today, it's all about living your best life – splurging on Instagram-worthy experiences, luxurious vacations and high-end tech. Saving for a rainy day? What's that? Sounds like a problem for Future You. But even in the YOLO age, there is a need for a soft voice whispering reminders that while you should absolutely enjoy the now, you still need to make sure tomorrow is not a financial train wreck.

I was hit with this realization at my son's second

birthday party. He had been to the birthday parties of all his friends and had seen the works – themed decorations, life-sized cartoon characters, tattoo corners and dessert tables straight out of Pinterest. Our first instinct was to throw that kind of party too. A fancy cake, a magic show, a DJ. Why not?

But it quickly turned into a tussle between my middle-class upbringing and modern-day realities. Eventually, I gave in and ended up spending around ₹30,000–40,000. Not a fortune, but definitely not a small sum either. As I stood there watching the celebration unfold, I couldn't help but think back to my own childhood birthdays. All we needed were a few balloons taped to the wall, a homemade cake and candles that we'd blow out with all the excitement in the world. It was simpler, sure, but the love and joy we were surrounded by were just as real.

This juxtaposition of then and now is not just a matter of nostalgia, but a reflection of how our relationship with money has evolved as a society. So whether you're team SST or YOLO, remember: money is a tool. It is essential for fulfilling your material needs and desires, both of which are shaped and influenced by the society we live in. The advantage we have is that there is meritocracy in the money game.

Tip: You can YOLO only if you're solo. If you have a family to take care of, their financial security needs to be a consideration when you are making financial decisions.

Meritocracy in the Money Game: A Tale of Two Titans

When it comes to the money game, few stories illustrate its highs and lows better than those of Radhakishan Damani and Vijay Mallya. Let's first talk about Radhakishan Damani – a legendary name in the Indian retail scene. Damani had humble beginnings, being born into a Marwari family in Bikaner, Rajasthan. He first dipped his toes into stockbroking and later, decided to dive into the retail world. In 2002, Damani launched his first D-Mart store in suburban Mumbai. His game plan was brilliant: keep things simple, offer quality products at prices that were easy on the pocket, and ditch the frills. His no-nonsense approach hit the sweet spot for India's middle class, who wanted value for money without having to compromise on quality.

So while everyone else was busy trying to take over the world overnight, Damani played it cool and adopted a slow and steady expansion strategy. He was extremely selective about where to open new stores, choosing spots in high-density residential areas to guarantee footfall. D-Mart started scaling up, even with big-name competitors lurking around. Damani truly got the Indian consumer. He understood that discounts and deals were not just an incentive but the main attraction. He cut out the middlemen and kept a tight grip on inventory, and this enabled D-Mart to offer affordable prices to its customers. Cut to today, D-Mart is a retail giant with hundreds of stores across India, and Damani is one of the richest in the country.

Compare this script to Vijay Mallya's, who inherited a legacy and turned it into a cautionary tale. Born into the wealthy Mallya family, he took over United Breweries Group (UB Group) at just twenty-eight. He turned UB Group into a global brand, especially with Kingfisher beer, which became the go-to beer brand in India. But Mallya could not content himself with just ruling the beer scene. In 2005, he launched Kingfisher Airlines with dreams of making it *the* luxury air travel brand in India. It started with a bang and the brand dazzled the market, but behind the scenes, cracks began forming.

The airline business, with its razor-thin margins and intense competition, is brutal. Kingfisher Airlines started racking up debt, thanks to sky-high operational costs and fierce competition. Mallya's personal penchant for luxury clouded his entrepreneurial decision-making. The debts kept mounting and by 2012, Kingfisher

Airlines was literally grounded. His financial troubles spiralled, leading to accusations of loan defaults and mismanagement. By 2016, he had fled to the UK, dodging legal battles and extradition attempts. Once known as the 'King of Good Times', Mallya's empire crumbled, leaving tough legal battles and unpaid loans in its wake.

These two stories could not be more different, yet they are very similar in what they serve to illustrate about the money game. Discipline wins. The real money game doesn't care about your starting point – it is about discipline, strategy and a willingness to learn. Being born into wealth and privilege is simply not enough; you will be rewarded only if you play the money game well and earn your stripes. But all this begs the golden question: How much money is enough?

Discovering Your Enough

Money, for me, has always been personal. It isn't a horse race where finishing first is all that matters. It is more like a toolkit to me, something that can help smooth out the bumps of life without turning me into a stress machine. Growing up in the '90s in a typical Indian middle-class family, I watched my parents stretch their budget to the very last rupee every month. We always made it work, and so the question of 'how much is enough?' has always played on my mind.

The basics are *roti, kapda aur makaan* (food, clothing and housing). If one has these essentials figured out, they can move on to securing other things in life. So for me, 'enough' means having the funds to take care of those basics, to put into investments to secure my family's future, to use for handling emergencies, and to maintain good health. Anything beyond that, I treat as extra sprinkles on the cupcake.

I went to college in the US on a scholarship, and like most international students, I was generally constrained when it came to money. Every dollar counted. Eating out was a luxury and budgeting was a necessity. My first two jobs in the US, first at McKinsey and then as a Wall Street analyst, changed that dramatically. I was suddenly earning more than I had ever imagined possible. And while I wasn't savvy enough to invest back then, I was a rigorous saver. And I mean *rigorous*.

Come 2009, I made an unpopular move. I quit a high-paying job to become an entrepreneur – a decision that felt financially questionable at the time, but ended up changing the course of my life completely. How could I do it? Well, firstly because I had the savings to fund my ambition and I didn't need to ask my family for help. So I didn't need to ask anybody for a loan or second-guess my choices because the money I had saved allowed me the freedom to take risks. The ability to make decisions like these are what make money meaningful. It is, after all, far more than just a number in your bank account. But just like numbers are infinite, so are our desires.

So what is enough for one person might not be for another. Your enough will always be personal. And the moment you start comparing it with anyone else's, you are setting yourself up for disappointment. I work in the financial services industry, where salaries are rarely a secret. What our former classmates and other counterparts elsewhere are earning is usually public information, thanks to various statutory regulations, headhunters and, of course, WhatsApp groups. If you start measuring your success against others', money can quickly become a source of unhappiness for you.

While I've done reasonably well in my career, I too had a very famous contemporary back in college. Guess who? Mark Zuckerberg. Will I ever be as wealthy as him? No chance. But that was never the point for me. My definition of enough was never about matching a billionaire's net worth – I cared far more about enjoying what I did, earning well and living a fulfilling life with people who make me happy.

There will always be someone richer and someone poorer than you. That's just how the world works. If you keep looking up, you might end up constantly feeling inadequate. If you only look down, you might end up becoming complacent. So play your own money game your way.

How, you ask? It all starts by learning all you can about money.

> **KEY LEARNINGS**
>
> - Build and nurture your relationship with money.
> - Find the right balance between YOLO and VFM to secure your future.
> - There is meritocracy in the money game. Believe in it.

2

MONEY 101

It's Part of Life's Syllabus

One Sunday morning, my mom strutted into the house from the market with bags of veggies in hand and a grin that could only mean one thing – she'd struck a good bargain. She plopped the bags on the counter and with a glint in her eye, announced, 'I got the tomatoes for ten rupees less, and the vendor even threw in some free dhania!'

Classic. This is the quintessential middle-class India – celebrating tiny victories at the veggie market ... while letting the big financial picture slide into the background. We derive so much pleasure from saving a few bucks on groceries, but saving to protect ourselves from inflation or retirement planning feels like worrying about distant clouds on a clear day to most of us.

I've tried talking to my mom about mutual funds, FDs, stocks and bonds, and every time, it feels to her like I am talking about something faraway and abstract. After all, none of that can beat the instant joy from saving a few rupees on veggies, right? But here's the thing: while we are busy haggling over a kilo of tomatoes, the real opportunities – the kind that can secure our future – are passing us by.

Imagine if we put the same energy into learning about investing? We'd be out here making our money work for us and not the other way around. But energy on its own is not sufficient. The highway to financial prosperity can be tricky to drive on. The headlights of financial knowledge are essential for helping us navigate the twists and turns in this journey. And to power those headlights, we need to learn about money.

The Cost of Ignorance

Rakesh, a schoolteacher from Kolkata, had been saving up for years to give his kids a secure future. Then came the Saradha Group, flashing promises of high returns like 15–50 per cent a year – way more than anything a regular investment could offer. Hooked onto the idea, Rakesh went all in with his life savings. At first, it seemed legit – he got the returns they had promised, so he even got his friends and family to jump on the bandwagon. The Saradha Group had big-name celebrities and politicians backing them, making everything appear genuine. Just like that, hundreds of thousands of people like Rakesh were drawn in.

Plot twist: Saradha turned out to be one giant

Ponzi scheme. They were just using money from new investors to pay off the old ones, so when the flow of new investments slowed, the whole thing came crashing down in 2013. The result? A financial nightmare for Rakesh and millions of others like him, who could have simply avoided falling for the scam if they had developed the financial awareness to recognize the Ponzi scheme for what it was. The first sign is an **unrealistic rate of returns**.

Financial scams are practically a sport in India. So knowing your way around money isn't just a skill that is good to have – it is essential for dodging financial disasters. Consider these staggering facts: In 2020–21, there were around 229 banking frauds happening every single day, according to the RBI. And in August 2022, over 200,000 depositors were duped out of a whopping ₹8,624 crore by shady non-banking firms running Ponzi schemes, as reported by the Economic Offences Wing of the Tamil Nadu Police. The bottom line? Not being money-smart can seriously mess you up, and there is way too much proof to ignore.

Increasing use of digital platforms for financial transactions is bound to worsen the problem even further. A massive surge in cybercrime incidents was reported in India in the last four years, with fraudsters cheating people out of ₹33,165 crore. According to the reports by National Cybercrime Reporting Portal (NCRP) under the Ministry of Home Affairs, around ₹551 crore were stolen in 2021, ₹2,306 crore in 2022,

₹7,496 crore in 2023 and a whopping ₹22,812 crore in 2024, with several Tier-2 and 3 cities being identified as cybercrime hotspots based on government data.

One of our friends, Mr Verma, was enjoying his life as a retiree in Pune at sixty. His financial needs were simple and he had no one else to take care of but himself. On a routine bank visit, he was sweet-talked by his relationship manager into buying a pricey life insurance policy. The advisor promised high returns and total security. Trusting the smooth pitch, Mr Verma signed up for the policy. But a few months into paying the hefty premiums, it hit him that the policy was totally unnecessary for someone in his shoes. The high returns were more like 'maybe' returns, and the scheme was better suited to someone with dependents. He realized he had been sold a dud. Mr Verma would have done well to fully understand the financial product before agreeing to purchase it – for which financial literacy is a crucial prerequisite.

Indians are highly vulnerable to persuasive sales tactics since such strategies appeal to one's emotions, even resorting to inciting a sense of fear and anxiety within you to push you to make quick decisions. Salespeople often crank up the pressure by listing all you might lose if you do not act *now*. And when they start throwing around jargon, it's easier to just give in than to dissect every claim. The key is to become aware of these moves so you can make smart decisions and avoid getting played.

I once had a conversation with a retired senior bureaucrat who was convinced the stock market was one big scam. Despite holding a top position in the government, he was very sceptical about the way the market operated. I could not help but point out the irony to him. 'Uncle,' I said, 'you work for the Government of India. It is the Bharat *sarkar* (government) that manages our economy, which is made up of the companies listed on the stock market. These companies are the ones driving our growth and progress.' After all, the stock market isn't some wild gambling den or *satta bazaar*. It is a regulated platform where businesses get the cash they need to grow and investors can earn a slice of the profits. The companies you see on the stock exchange are the ones contributing to our country's Gross Domestic Product (GDP), creating jobs and driving innovation.

Thus, financial literacy is the key to busting some of the common money myths going around out there. In India, we are prone to swinging between two extremes – either we think that the stock markets are totally rigged, or that they're a golden ticket to instant wealth. Yes, scams may have happened in the past, but it is not all doom and gloom. The truth lies somewhere in the middle, and it has the power to set you free, provided you are willing to dive in and learn for yourself. Mistrust usually stems from stories about big losses and crazy volatility – which are also sensational and make for interesting news – than stories of people applying smart money management skills in the market to create a pathway to building wealth in the long term. When you learn about money, you make decisions based on facts, rather than as a victim of dramatic news, misinformation and emotional manipulation.

Financial Fundamentals You Need to Know

Back in 2018, Raj, one of our mutual friends, called me up in full panic mode. Despite earning a hefty monthly paycheck, he was drowning in debt. He had taken out a massive personal loan to throw into stocks, lured in by his 'friends' making promises of quick, easy money. Raj didn't have a fallback plan to pay it off on his own, should he have to; he was banking solely on the stock market to magically make it all go away. With 'friends' like these ... by now you know how it goes.

Spoiler alert: the market tanked. Instead of rolling in cash, Raj found himself being hounded by bankers. Non-stop calls and messages from recovery agents really messed with Raj's head. Every time his phone rang or a letter showed up, his anxiety spiked, plunging his mental health and self-esteem into a pit. He started ghosting everyone, too embarrassed to hang out or even talk to friends and family.

Keen to help Raj out, we gave him sound financial advice and all the emotional support we could muster. We got on the phone with the agencies, hashed out a repayment plan that Raj could actually stick to, and slowly got him back on track. Raj's experience was yet another example of why one needed to be smart about spending, saving, investing and borrowing, and how all it took was one wrong move for things to completely spiral out of control.

Personal finance boils down to five main activities: **earning, spending, saving, investing** and **borrowing**. **Smart spending** means knowing what is worth your money and what is not. Prioritizing your expenses does not mean being miserly. **Regular saving** is your safety net for emergencies or for future goals. **Investing** is where the magic happens, making your money work and grow. **Borrowing**, if done right, can help you level up but if you go overboard, you're looking at a debt disaster.

Balancing these is like playing a game of Jenga – everything needs to be in perfect balance. Sure, earning well is great, but that's just 40–50 per cent of the game. The real challenge is learning to manage spending, saving, investing and borrowing.

The Time Is Now

So when are you ready to start learning about money? The earlier you start, the better. We are not taught anything about managing finances at school, so most of us are left to figure it out on our own as and when the need arises in life. Many of us feel that unless a certain field of education will land us our dream job, we simply don't need to learn it. But think about what might have been if you didn't learn to read and write in school. You don't have to aspire to be the next Shakespeare to learn how to write – it is a basic skill everyone should have. The same applies to money. Financial literacy is not just a must for future economists, but for every mango person.

It is also important to learn from the right sources. According to a 2019 survey by the National Centre for Financial Education (NCFE), only 27 per cent of Indian adults were financially literate. Compare that to Western countries where the rates are way higher – like 57 per cent in the US and about 66 per cent in Germany. After the demonetization in 2016, the Indian government has been promoting digital financial literacy. The Reserve Bank of India (RBI) even organizes Financial Literacy Week to spread awareness about the key topics related to money; in 2023, the theme was 'Good Financial Behaviour – Your Saviour'. You can learn more about various financial products on the SEBI Investor portal and other reliable online and offline resources, as Ananya did.

A few years ago, my friend Ananya, a busy working mom, wanted to start learning about handling her finances. I suggested she start small – like just fourteen minutes a day. She got into the groove of reading short finance articles, watching budgeting videos and listening to investment podcasts after tucking her kids into bed.

A month later, Ananya was already feeling the change. She felt way more in control of and confident about dealing with her money. Just by carving out a little bit of time each day, she had learned about emergency funds, compound interest and low-cost index funds. A year later, Ananya had clocked in over eighty-five hours of financial know-how. She was managing her money better, growing her wealth and being a financial role model for her kids.

My tip to Ananya was based on the Rule of 100, which says that if you dedicate 100 minutes a week to learning something, you'll see serious improvement over time. That's just fourteen minutes a day. Very manageable and easy to remain consistent with. And it works! The tiny steps add up to major gains in financial smarts.

Ananya's story shows that learning about money doesn't have to be a time-sucking vampire. Small, steady efforts can lead to big changes. Becoming money-savvy empowers you to chase your dreams. For example, if you're earning a salary and want to buy a house, it might seem impossible with today's crazy real estate prices. But the truth is that smart saving and investing can help you turn that dream into a reality. Such is the magic of financial literacy – it is the wind under your sails propelling you towards the shores of wealth.

Tip: Financial literacy is the gateway to financial prosperity.

The Non-Essentials: What You Don't Need to Learn

Here's the good news: You don't need to know it all.

While my dad and brother are all about trading stocks, my mom and sister-in-law are usually reluctant to get involved. One evening, the men were deep in conversation about their latest trades, and my mom and sister-in-law were just sitting there, completely lost. My dad was diving into the nitty gritties of some market trend, while my brother was sharing his two cents on some tech stock.

At some point, my mom chimed in with 'This is why I don't mess with money. I don't have time to keep up with the stock market every day.'

This is a classic example of why so many people, especially women, shy away from taking charge of their finances. They think they need to be glued to the news and master stock trading. But here's the thing: managing your money doesn't have to be complicated. You don't need to be a stock market whiz or check your investments daily to get started. Women, in particular, need to ditch the idea that finance is too tricky or time-consuming for them to bother with it. The basics of personal finance are easy to grasp and do not require you to become an expert.

A good place to start? Budgeting, saving and discovering the magic of compound interest. Those are the real game-changers. Financial independence is merely a matter of making simple, smart decisions that fit your lifestyle; not trying to become a pro overnight. After all, you don't need to be a MasterChef to whip up a meal for yourself – just the basics would suffice.

You are now ready to take the first step: saving.

> **KEY LEARNINGS**
>
> - Personal finance has five aspects: **earning, spending, saving, investing** and **borrowing**.
> - You don't have to become an expert: start making smart financial decisions by learning about **budgeting, saving** and **compound interest**.
> - Apply the Rule of 100 and save fourteen minutes each day to learn about basic financial concepts.

References

- Ashok Upadhyay, '229 banking frauds a day in 2020-21, recovery rate below 1%, RBI says in RTI reply', *India Today*, 15 December 2021. Available at: https://www.indiatoday.in/business/story/229-banking-frauds-day-2020-21-recovery-rate-rbi-rti-reply-1888096-2021-12-15.
- R. Sivaraman, 'Over 2 lakh depositors cheated of ₹8,640 crore in Ponzi scheme', *The Hindu*, 10 August 2022. Available at: https://www.thehindu.com/news/cities/chennai/over-2-lakh-depositors-cheated-of-8640-crore-in-ponzi-scheme/article65754001.ece.

- Mahender Singh Manral, 'Cyber frauds jump 900% in 4 years: Small cities like Deoghar, Nuh, Mathura emerge as new scam Capitals', *The Indian Express*, 5 February 2025. Available at: https://indianexpress.com/article/india/cybercrime-sharp-rise-complaints-2024-govt-data-9816845/.

Resources

- SEBI Investor portal. Available at: https://investor.sebi.gov.in/.

3

SAVING VERSUS INVESTING

Fuelling Up to Hit the Road

In the world of motorsport, Rajveer Singh – better known as RV – was a name synonymous with speed. With podium finishes in every race and earnings more than most could dream of, he lived life in the fast lane both on and off the track. Sleek cars, a luxurious home, a perfect family – he had it all. His financial strategy for attaining his goals was simple: Borrow now, pay later. Every aspect of his lifestyle was funded by Equated Monthly Instalments or EMIs. When his wife, Priya, asked RV to exercise caution, he would use one of his hands like an imaginary knife to cut portions on his other palm in response, referring to how he was 'dividing up' the expense into EMIs.

RV's racing career fuelled his spending habits. But fate had a different plan. One overcast day, a split-second misjudgement sent his car spinning off the track.

RV's career ended in an instant. The stream of income dried up almost overnight. Financial strain eventually forced him into bankruptcy. The debts he once managed so comfortably now became unmanageable and all the possessions he had purchased on EMIs had to be auctioned off to pay his outstanding debt – from cars to watches to even their family home.

'But they can't auction our home!' RV argued.

Priya nodded and that was enough to tell him that they could – and so they did. RV had underestimated the consequences of not being able to meet financial obligations. The family was uprooted and had to move from their dream home to a tiny room in a slum. Priya had to work multiple jobs just to put food on the table. It took immense effort – and a near-miracle – for RV to regain his confidence and get his life back on track. Sound familiar? This is the plot of *Ta Ra Rum Pum* (2007), starring Saif Ali Khan and Rani Mukherjee, an underrated Bollywood gem that teaches an important financial lesson amidst all the entertainment.

The lesson: Financial stability is not a luxury; it is a necessity – while living for today is important, so is planning for tomorrow. Prudent financial planning is a game of balancing both halves: **saving** and **investing**. Understanding the distinction between and the significance of both can save you from skidding into RV's situation.

Saving vs. Investing

A young girl, barely in her teens, was on a cricket ground, practising her shots under the supervision of India's former legendary captain, MS Dhoni. Thala, as he is fondly called, was patiently making sure the girl's posture was spot-on and her elbow was in the right position when striking the shot. The girl's father was watching from a distance and his heart swelled with pride when another cricketing legend, Sachin Tendulkar, came along and praised the girl's talent. He walked over to them. 'She wants to play for India when she grows up,' he said. 'I'm saving for her future already.'

'If the goal is to secure the child's future,' Sachin said, '*toh maidan mein utarna hoga* (then you will need to step onto the playing field).'

The father looked puzzled until Dhoni stepped in to explain. The field the father needed to play in was not the cricket ground – it was investments. 'Saving is important, but savings alone aren't enough. The money you save stagnates. Instead, consider investing in mutual funds and help your money grow.' He goes on to explain to the girl's father how professional cricket coaching is an expensive pursuit. If he relied solely on saving in FDs, which grow at a mere 6–7 per cent, he would eventually lose the battle to the 5–6 per cent rate of inflation and taxes due on income. By investing in market-linked instruments, however, his savings stood a better chance of growing at a pace that could match or even outpace inflation.

So just as cricketers must step onto the field to win matches, one must translate at least part of their savings into investment to see actual growth.

The above scene was originally part of a script for an advertisement by the Association of Mutual Funds in India (AMFI), aimed at increasing awareness about mutual funds. It truly drives home the difference between savings and investing through an effective example. It is important to invest rather than to merely set aside money in savings. But for investing, one needs capital. And for capital, one needs savings. So what is the best way to save money?

The Savings Framework

At a recent investors' event in Pune, where I was invited to speak, a young twenty-five-year-old professional stood up to ask me question that is often asked across social media and in casual conversations about money:

'How can I save money?' he said, his voice echoing through the hall. 'Between home loans, food delivery apps and exotic vacations, how on earth can *anyone* save money?'

The audience murmured in agreement, relating hard to the young man's predicament.

'If you want to improve at cricket,' I said, 'go for net practice.'

'Practice in the nets?' he asked, puzzled by my cricket analogy.

'Exactly.' I explained how saving is like net practice. It helps you hone the discipline for money management. Investing, on the other hand, can be compared to playing the actual match. Naturally, one cannot be done without mastering the other. The runs you score and the goals you achieve.

To get started with the practice of saving, I recommended the **10-30-50** framework to him.

Between twenty to thirty years of age, you can safely aim to stow away at least **10 per cent** of your income. Sound like a buzzkill? Understandable. For the young and carefree who have just started earning, saving isn't always a top priority. Salary packages or earnings are comparatively lower in the early part of one's career, and branded jeans and shoes beckon from dazzling displays in malls. Certain movies *must* be watched in theatres, where the popcorn costs more than the tickets. Sure, it's good to enjoy it all while you can, but you must also remember that some smart planning between your twenties and thirties can help you build sturdy foundations for your future.

Think of it as paying your future self – and trust me, future you will be thankful. Big time. Create an emergency fund that covers six months to one year of your expenses. Plan for short-term goals, even if it is just buying those expensive sneakers you've been eyeing.

Between your thirties–forties, your money inflow will

increase. You will receive those coveted promotions (or you'll move jobs for a good hike, won't you?), or maybe your business will grow. Start saving at least **30 per cent** of your income around this time. You'll probably be married or have plans to walk down the aisle by then, or you may have made a down payment on a home, or just have plans of doing so. This is a good time to start investing for those long-term goals.

By the time you are on the other side of the big F – your forties onwards – you'll be earning at your peak potential. Scary expenses like a higher education for your kids and your looming retirement are sure to cross your mind. You can now start planning for these. Try to save at least **50 per cent** of your income at this stage.

While the 10-30-50 framework begins with a saving rate of 10 per cent, which is fairly achievable when one has just started earning, it is normal to feel apprehensive. If the 10 per cent mark makes you feel too jittery, start with saving just 1 per cent and slowly increase this amount over a period of time.

Tip: Savings is a habit-driven approach. Initially, forming the habit of saving is more important than the percentage of money you save.

An Easy Savings Hack

Any system which is automated or mandated becomes difficult to bypass. For example, the process of TDS or Tax Deducted at Source, makes it challenging for taxpayers to evade taxes by making the mandatory deductions before the money hits your bank account. You're never late for paying your taxes because the government deducts them directly from your income before it even gets into your hands.

Now what if you could replicate this for your savings? Imagine an automated savings system called **SDS** (Savings Deducted at Source), which would deduct a fixed amount from our earnings and automatically redirect it to a Systematic Investment Plan (SIP), Recurring Deposit (RD) or FD before we get a chance to spend it. When part of your money is saved before you get a chance to see it, you're less likely to feel its absence or spend it impulsively. It's like having a financial autopilot to steer you towards your goals. Wouldn't that be an easy, powerful hack?

For salaried individuals

If you have a regular, predictable income, automating a budget for savings is easy and straightforward. Start by fixing the amount you'd like to save and set up an automated transfer into your SDS system.

BEWARE OF DEBT

Debt and credit cards can throw your savings plans off track. Carrying your credit card around in your wallet makes it too easy to swipe without thinking if you can't resist the temptation. Higher credit limits provide a false fake sense of enhanced spending power. But a credit limit of ₹2 lakh does not mean you *have* ₹2 lakh to spend – it only means that you can now potentially run up a credit card bill of up to 2 lakh, which you will still need to pay back to the bank at the end of the month. Hence, a good thumb rule is to remember to **limit your credit card spending to a sum you can comfortably pay off in full at the end of your billing cycle without disrupting your SDS.**

For entrepreneurs, freelancers and gig workers

If you do not have fixed income streams, budgeting becomes important. Automation of savings may not be practical for you. The following might be more helpful to help you save:

- **Set manual targets:** Instead of monthly goals, fix suitable periodic goals, such as a quarterly or semi-annual savings budget, based on your earnings.

- **Create buffer months:** Allocate months where you can save more aggressively. Preferably, do this during months when your income is higher than average, as it will help you build a surplus that can average out the leaner months.
- **Track and adjust:** Regularly review your earnings and adjust your savings goals as needed.

On to Investing

Recently, my mother and I were invited to a wedding in the family where I had the opportunity to observe just how much our spending habits had changed as a society over the last few decades. Once she was ready, she slipped on a gold bangle she had purchased decades ago and made a casual but poignant observation that stayed with me for the rest of the night. 'In our days,' she said, 'everyone could purchase gold sets quite easily. Now it's difficult to even buy one bangle.'

When we arrived at the venue, it was clear that the groom's family, who had invited us, had spared no expense. Towering floral arrangements adorned the entrance. Crystal chandeliers cast a gentle glow over the silk-draped tables. A live band played some jazz, as servers floated around offering gourmet appetizers and fancy drinks. Food stations had everything from sushi to more than 250 desi delicacies. Celebrities and social media influencers were mingling with business moguls, as their designer outfits glittered under the lights. The grand finale was nothing short of a spectacle.

Remembering her own wedding, my mother said, 'Your dad and I got married in a small park in a narrow lane. Unimaginable these days.'

And then it struck me – she was absolutely right! It is not just the price of gold, or food, or wedding venues which has gone up owing to **financial inflation**, but also our aspirations – what we want for ourselves and our families, pushing us to aim for more money so we can improve our purchasing power. This can be called **aspirational inflation**, which is inevitable, usually much more and notoriously hard to keep track of.

If aspirations are growing and so are the prices of commodities, then your savings also need to grow in equal proportion. If inflation keeps growing but our money doesn't, the gap between what we earn and what we want only widens. Fortunately, we receive cash flows from salaries, bonuses, business deals and sale of assets. With the right investments, we can beat financial inflation and also keep pace with our aspirational inflation through investing part of our savings. Investing enables you to make more money off your savings and create wealth in the long run. If done well, it is a surefire way of ensuring you can afford the things you dream of, whether it entails buying gold, hosting a lavish wedding, or simply living a life free of financial stress.

So where can you start?

The Investment Framework

Investing is a deeply personal journey, and no one solution works the same for every investor. At another conference where I was the guest speaker, I was taking questions on investments. A member of the audience asked me whether he should start a SIP or invest in gold. While the intent behind the question was right, it was fundamentally the wrong question to ask. It is like a parent wondering whether their child should go to Harvard University or Film and Technology Institute, Pune, even before evaluating their academic interests, career goals or their own financial capacity.

Investment choices are personal because they are a reflection of our individual goals, personality and circumstances. Each person's strategy is shaped by their life experiences, values and aspirations.

Consider this: a friend of mine had seen his father's business capsize under the weight of a high-interest loan. This caused him to develop a lifelong aversion to debt. On the other hand, I have a fairly comfortable equation with loans because my profession offers predictable income, making it easier for me to have a more realistic understanding of the kind of debt I can afford. No two investment plans can be exactly alike and work well for all people, making it deeply important to tailor the process of investing your money to meet your needs.

Before making investment choices, you should know the three factors which influence them. And you can remember them using the Oscar-winning song, '*Naatu Naatu*'.

RRR: Runway, Risk, Returns

- **Runway:** This refers to the amount of time you have until you need your money. Time is one of the most critical factors in choosing investment instruments because it determines how you can best navigate the ups and downs of the market. So start by considering how soon you might need access to your money to hit that financial goal. Investments with higher liquidity are preferable for short-term needs. If you will need the amount you have set aside to invest in the near future, say in about one to two years, it is best to avoid high-risk, high-return products to ensure your capital remains safe until you need it. Conversely, for the long term – for goals that are years or decades away (eg. retirement) – you can afford to take more risks and generate higher returns, as detailed in later chapters.

Tip: Avoid locking your money in long-term investments if you anticipate that you will need to withdraw it sooner than the stipulated period.

- **Risk**: The uncertainty of returns is called risk. All investments carry some amount of risk but it varies significantly across different types of investments. To understand risk better, it is important to understand three key concepts:
  - *Risk tolerance* is your emotional capacity and willingness to endure market fluctuations. This is influenced by your past experience, age and financial wisdom. Younger investors often have a higher risk tolerance because they have more time to recover from potential losses.
  - *Risk capacity* is your financial ability to take risks, based on your income, savings and other assets. Even if you are mentally prepared to take higher risks, your financial situation might not support it.
  - *Diversification* is the practice of investing in multiple types of investment instruments in order to offset the impact of any single investment's poor performance. A well-diversified portfolio typically includes a mix of stocks, bonds and other assets.

    As a thumb rule, you can preserve your capital by opting for low-risk instruments. It is also wise to spread your investments across various asset classes to mitigate risk. Avoid overexposing yourself to high-risk instruments if it jeopardizes your sense of financial stability.
- **Returns**: Returns are the outcome of your investment decisions, influenced by both runway and risk

tolerance. While it may be tempting to chase high returns, it often leads to excessive risk-taking, which can backfire. High returns are an outcome of the time you have and the level of risk you are willing to take. **Set realistic return expectations** by basing your assessment purely on performance histories and the current market conditions. Also focus on **balancing your return goals with your risk tolerance**.

In a nutshell:
- For short-term goals, like upgrades or other purchases, opt for a short runway, low risk and moderate returns from among the available options to help you maintain liquidity. This way, your money will remain safe and accessible for when you might need it.
- For long-term goals, like retirement planning, opt for long runways, higher risk and high-returns products. This will help you grow your capital without worrying about recovering the losses you endure due to short-term market fluctuations.

By following this framework, you can make more informed decisions and enhance the likelihood of you achieving your financial objectives. Investing is not a one-size-fits-all endeavour and understanding the **RRR** (Runway, Risk, Returns) framework will empower you to create a strategy that works for you. Maybe listening to '*Naatu Naatu*' will incite even more joy now! After all, it is the map that leads to the key to understanding investment: Runway, Risk and Returns.

When to Start Your Money Journey?

Whoever you are, wherever you are, the right time for you to start investing is *now*. When I was in school, we used to sing the national anthem every day, although I never quite knew what the lyrics meant. Originally composed in Bengali with Sanskrit words sprinkled in, it was beyond the comprehension of any child at that age. Yet, I used to sing it with full fervour. I learned it by heart through sheer repetition. It became a habit.

Saving money is a lot like learning the national anthem – at a fundamental level, it is about forming a habit. It takes time, consistency and regular practice to incorporate these crucial learnings into your lifestyle. Research suggests it takes about twenty-one days to form a new habit. But since most of us tend to look at savings as a monthly exercise, you should aim to save consistently for twenty-one months for it to become a way of life. It does not matter how much you start with – saving is a discipline and to master it, you need to do it regularly. The longer you stick with it, the stronger the habit becomes – and the higher the rewards! A *doha* by Sant Kabir comes to mind, for it truly embodies how the practice of savings becomes a habit:

Karat-karat abhyas ke, jadmati hot sujan.
Rasari aavat jaat te, sil par padat nishan.

(Through regular practice, even a dull mind can become wise.
Even a rope can leave its mark on a rock just by repeatedly rubbing against it.)

KEY LEARNINGS

- Investing your money can help you beat inflation.
- To start investing, you need to save up capital. You can do this using the 10-30-50 framework.
- You can also automate savings through an SDS system.
- Once you learn to save, graduate to investing that savings.
- To start investing and know what investment product is right for your individual needs, use the RRR framework.
- Remember: saving is a habit you need to train with discipline.

4

DEBT

A Friend in Need, a Foe in Greed

Debt is like the hole that is sure to sink a ship. Take the example of Big Bazaar – the quintessential retail success story. Launched in 2001, it became the go-to shopping destination for buyers across India. Its stores mirrored the chaotic charm of local bazaars, establishing a deep connection with customers. Kishor Biyani, the visionary behind Future Group, became a giant in retail, employing over 30,000 people to manage 12 million square feet of retail space across 1,500 stores across 400+ cities. At its peak in 2019, just before the pandemic, Future group reported a revenue of ₹30,524 crore.

But then things got messy. Unlike other Indian retail chains that minimized short-term loans and reinvested profits, Biyani relied heavily on short-term borrowing to rapidly expand and diversify into various sectors. In the face of competition from larger conglomerates, his own aggressive borrowing and the COVID-19 pandemic, the Future Group failed to hold its own. Sales plummeted, bankers started demanding repayments and foreign capital completely dried up and Big Bazaar was forced to shut shop.

Years later, reflecting on the Big Bazaar journey as a guest on a podcast, Biyani lamented that the FDI regulations prevailing at the time did not allow him to bring in as much foreign capital into the business as he would have liked. When the COVID-19 pandemic struck, he lost a whopping ₹7,000 crores and bouncing back from that was nearly impossible. Running purely on bank loans, he had already been in too tight a spot. 'Then we decided,' said Biyani, 'there was no other option but to settle and sell out.'

Debt dealt the fatal blow to Big Bazaar, but it was also the most formidable weapon in its armory that had propelled it to great heights for many years. Confusing, isn't it? Let us try and unpack that.

Debt: A Double-edged Sword

In 1957, a remote Indian village was celebrating the completion of an irrigation canal – a symbol of hope for its prosperity. Radha, a revered maternal figure in the village, was invited to inaugurate it. She recalled her past on the momentous occasion – her grand wedding to Shamu, funded using a ₹500 loan from the greedy moneylender, Sukhilala, whose cruelty and harsh lending terms forced the young couple to surrender most of their harvest and saddled them with considerable debt. Sukhilala's exploitative ways in Mehboob Khan's iconic film *Mother India* (1957) remains one of Indian cinema's sharpest depictions of the devastating impact of debt on people's lives..

For decades, debt has remained a recurring theme in Indian cinema as a source of strife and suffering – at least until the '90s. We've seen it all on the silver screen – homes auctioned, cars confiscated and businesses destroyed by this one evil force of *karza* (debt). In a way, we still see it like that. Debt is a monthly outflow of your income that brings along two unwanted guests: first is the **interest** component, which is often very high. Second is the ticking timebomb outlined in the loan agreement: the **due date**.

Debt is like a leaky bucket draining your finances every month; EMIs are like swords dangling over your head all the time. Every rupee you try to plug the leak with is a rupee that cannot be saved. And if, God forbid, life throws an unexpected curveball at you during this time, it can seriously strain your mental health and reduce the overall quality of your life.

A mountain of wealth cannot be built over a pit of debt. You'll always find yourself scrambling to fill up that hole if you need to frequently take out loans to support your lifestyle. Now that loans have become even easier to access, it can be tempting to aspire to a lifestyle you can't realistically afford with your current finances, but going down that road will only lead you deeper into that pit of debt. The truth is, even if you're doing it just to impress others, there's no glory in it if it comes at the cost of your own financial well-being. Today, seven out of ten iPhones in India are bought on EMIs. As the great American humorist Will Rogers has famously stated, 'Too many people spend money they haven't earned, to buy things they don't want, to impress people that they don't like.'

Listen to Rogers. Don't be one of those people.

Good and Bad Debt

So did we scare you? Or did we scare you? Of course, that was not our intent – we want to educate and inform you, not intimidate. Now that you are aware of the dangers of debt, you can heave a sigh of relief. But here comes the plot twist: debt is not always bad!

Good debt (yes, it exists) can help with growth in your life. Such debt is typically incurred for assets that can appreciate in value or generate income over time. When you take out a loan to purchase a home which will appreciate in value and provide a stable living space, that is good debt. There are also tax benefits to be gained from such debt. Similarly, a loan to start or expand a profitable business is also good, although it is good practice to ensure that 100 per cent of your capital is not coming from debt. Investing in higher education which can enhance your earnings potential in the future, such as an MBA, is also good debt. Good debt is generally meant to fund your *needs* and include purchases or investments that can contribute to long-term growth and financial security.

Bad debt will generally finance your *wants*. Accumulating credit card debt by making only the 'minimum due' payments, personal loans for exotic vacations, or for purchasing expensive gadgets – all constitute bad debt.

Understanding the difference between good and bad debt is fundamental to effective personal finance management.

The RATE Framework

Here is a framework to help you differentiate between good and bad debt.

- **R (Rate of Interest)**: Think of this as the price tag on your debt. Lower rate = better deal. Home loans and education loans often have low interest rates.
- **A (Appreciation Potential)**: If what you are borrowing for is likely to go up in value over time, that is a win. Buying commercial property that'll appreciate is smarter than splurging on a high-end fancy car that starts losing value from the moment you drive it out of the showroom.
- **T (Term of Repayment)**: The quicker you pay it off, the less you'll end up shelling out in interest. Shorter terms might pinch your pocket in the moment, but

they save you big money (interest) in the long run.
- **E (Earnings Potential):** If your loan helps you make more money, it's golden. Borrowing for a laptop you need for work? Smart. But financing a new phone just because it has an extra inch of screen size? Not so much.

If you remember to check for these four factors before deciding whether or not to take on a certain debt, you can handle it like a pro. **Remember: Even the best debt can turn bad if you do not stay on top of it. Balance your debt with your income, stick to a fixed budget and keep your financial game going strong.** Now that you know about good and bad debt, you are ready to learn how to evaluate whether you can afford debt – even if it is good.

Debt Affordability Framework

A debt affordability framework is your personal yardstick for figuring out if you can handle debt without messing up your finances. There's no one-size-fits-all formula for this, unfortunately, but there are some key indicators and ratios that can be used to check if a debt has the potential to throw a wrench in your financial plans. The **30:3:6 Debt Affordability Framework** is one such tool. It covers three aspects:
- **Debt-to-Income Ratio:** Your EMI should be **under 30 per cent** of your monthly income. If more than a

third of your paycheck is going towards paying for your debts, it's time to pull the brakes.
- **Total Debt:** Your total debt should not be more than **three times** your annual income. Anything above that figure is sure to entrap you.
- **Emergency Funds:** You should ideally keep **6 months'** worth of EMIs stashed away in an emergency fund. If you don't have some kind of a backup plan to get out of your current debt, adding more is a no-go.

For large debts like a home loan, get yourself an insurance policy. This way, if life takes an unexpected turn, your family won't get stuck in a debt spiral.

But being able to afford debt does not guarantee that institutional lenders will be willing to lend to you. Have you ever applied for a loan and discovered that your application was rejected? If yes, it may have had something to do with your credit score.

Your Credit Score and How You Can Improve It

In an episode of *Shark Tank India*, Priyasha Saluja from The Cinnamon Kitchen made a pitch to raise funds for her gluten-free goodies business. Just when one of the 'sharks' Aman Gupta, co-founder of boAt, was about to back out from the deal, Priyasha mentioned her stellar credit score: 838. And guess what? She landed the deal!

The budding entrepreneurs out there must take note: a good credit score can be your ticket not just to the right loan, but also attract investors to your business. If you keep that score in check, who knows, you might get lucky and find me amongst the sharks again in another season to hand you your dream deal!

What Is a Credit Score?

Your credit score is a number that shows how well you've managed your money and debts over time – how promptly you paid your EMIs, cleared your credit card bills, and also how frequently you have used these instruments. This is based on data from credit reports recorded by credit bureaus, and the higher your score, the more trustworthy you look to lenders. It's like scoring an A+ in financial responsibility, causing lenders to trust you more readily with loans. In India, the most popular credit score is the CIBIL score, which ranges from 300 to 900 and ratings from poor to excellent.

CIBIL Score Range	Rating
300–499	Poor
500–649	Average
650–749	Good
750–900	Excellent

Your borrowing and repaying habits play a major role in determining your credit score. Some practices that can help you enhance your scores and get that loan application approved without a hitch include:

- Paying off loans and credit card bills on time.
- Keeping your balances well below your credit limit.
- A longer history of making these payments on time.
- Having different types of credit (like credit cards, car loans, etc.) to your name can also be a plus, although opening a lot of new loan accounts too quickly can dent your score for a bit.

Tip: Keep your credit score in the 750–900 range.

What if you have already made the juvenile mistake of not paying your credit card bills on time in your twenties? What if you haven't paid the several EMIs due on that expensive car you purchased? All of these will affect your credit score and are also signs that you have inadvertently entered the financial *chakravyuh*.

However, there is a way out.

How to Get Out of the Debt Trap

In *Mahabharata*, the chakravyuh was a complex, spiral military formation designed to trap anyone who dared to enter it. Experienced warriors like Arjuna, however, were equipped with the military wisdom to not only enter but also safely exit such a formation. Similarly, you too can be equipped to get out of the debt trap.

Start by taking a good look at your debts – credit card bills, personal loans, student loans, you name it. Add them all up and see how much you owe in total. Check the interest rates on each and focus on the high-interest ones first – those are the deadly ones.

Next, craft a game plan to track every rupee you spend. This will help you assess where there is room for you to cut back. Maybe take a break from those daily lattes for a bit? Then decide how much you can realistically direct towards your debt each month. Tackle the highest-interest debt first, or start with the smallest debt to get some quick wins under your belt. Both methods work well.

If juggling multiple debts makes your head spin, consolidate them into one loan with a lower interest rate. It may make sense to use a personal loan to pay off the outstanding on your credit card in full due to low interest rates of the former. Then cut the credit card in two with a pair of scissors (*do not skip this step*) and focus on repaying the personal loan.

Once you're finally on track, stick to your budget and avoid taking on any new debt. The more you practise mindful spending, the better you will be at keeping your finances in check. Keep pushing forward and you'll soon be standing on solid financial ground.

Remember, debt is not bad if it is under your control. At the gym, you should lift as much weight as you can control. Lifting more weight than you can bear is likely to cause injury. Similarly, debt you cannot afford forces you into a debt trap, coming out of which takes time and discipline. But with the right approach, it can be done. It is important to celebrate small victories and stay motivated along the way. And when you've started making payments on time, go ahead and order that latte. One for me, too!

> **KEY LEARNINGS**
>
> - There is good debt and bad debt. Good debt meets your needs, and bad debt is for your wants.
> - Use the RATE framework to evaluate good vs. bad debt.
> - Use the 30:3:6 Debt Affordability Framework to decide if you can afford debt.
> - Avoid debt traps completely.
> - If you're already in a debt trap, improving your spending habits is your ticket to the way out.

5

RISK

Don't Buy a Ticket to the Wrong Ride

Have you ever rolled your eyes when they check your boarding pass multiple times before you are allowed to occupy your seat on a flight? Once when you go through the security check, then at the boarding gate, where it is checked two more times – just as you enter the boarding area and then again just before you step onto the aircraft. Of course, these stringent security checks can be frustrating at times, but they are necessary to keep all of us safe in the skies. Flying is way safer now than it used to be. Back in the '70s, there were about 4.2 plane crashes per million flights, but now they're down to just 0.13. That's almost a 97 per cent drop! Statistically, flying is now one of the safest things you can do. The chances of you dying on a flight are a minuscule one in 11 million. To put it into perspective: you are more likely to be struck by lightning than die in a plane crash.

So what has curtailed the risks of flying? You guessed it right – the 'frustrating' safety protocols that the aviation industry has introduced and improved over the years have played the biggest role. But despite all these measures and the impressive stats, some people are still terrified of flying. But in this time and age, the way it is likely that you'll board at least one flight in your lifetime, if not more, because it is an essential and convenient mode of transport. It is best to learn and overcome one's fears because flying is here to stay.

Similarly, there are people who are terrified of investing because of a vague sense of risk. And like flying, investing too has become an essential skill to navigate modern life. The one proven way you can overcome your fears about it is by learning to manage the risks.

Risk, put simply, is the question mark in front of the chances of losing your money. It is a crucial part of the investing game. If you take the time to understand it properly, you can apply your skills to level up your returns!

Thrilling or Chilling? Take Your Pick

Why do amusement park rides range from a chill carousel with its smooth, slow circular ride to the wild rollercoaster with epic twists and that stomach-wrenching drop?

So that everyone who visits the park can have a good time!

The creators understand that a good time can mean different things to different people and so there are options for everyone to enjoy. But once you buy the ticket, you are in-charge of designing your own individual experience in the park.

You could go for the carousel – a safer bet; low-risk but also low-thrill. Or you could go for the rollercoaster – a bit of a gamble; there's a slight chance that you might end up with your head spinning. Then there is the option between the two – a ferris wheel. It is not as wild as the rollercoaster, but not as slow as the carousel either. Your preferences are entirely personal, based on your own comfort level. Apply the same principle to investing.

It is essential that you take only as much risk as you are comfortable taking. The right amount of risk will help you achieve your goals without losing a good night's sleep. Good money management, after all, is all about taking calculated risks. The risk–return trade-off is that higher rewards typically come from bigger risks. But just like the rides at the amusement park, all kinds of investments can deliver surprises. Not every high-risk investment will deliver sky-high returns, and sometimes, low-key carousels can surprise you with better-than-expected performance. In financial jargon, we call this risk-adjusted returns. For example, two investments might both have a 10 per cent return, but if one is much riskier than the other, the less risky investment is considered as having a better risk-adjusted return. And when it comes to investing, there are factors which can help us identify such risks from the outset.

Tip: Risk is like fire. Controlled, it can cook you a meal; unchecked, it can burn down your house. Manage it wisely.

Different Types of Risk in Investing

At the amusement park, we often get scared because of various kinds of risks posed by the various rides, and this is mostly due to our perception that it is unidimensional. But that's simply not true. There are levels to risks and it is important to know the triggers behind our fears: is it that the ride goes really fast, really high, or through dark tunnels and narrow passages? Personally, I am not as scared of the fast ones as I am of heights, so I avoid the ones I won't enjoy accordingly. Similarly, once you start recognizing and analysing different kinds of risks involved in every offering, you'll know better which ones to avoid.

Have you heard of people struggling to sell their property because they are in immediate need of cash? I saw three different acquaintances of mine go through it. They owned plenty of real estate but when they needed liquid funds on short notice, they found themselves in a tight spot. In one case, the tenants refused to move out. In another, the property prices of the area where they lived had dropped due to the area getting flooded frequently, making it hard for them to sell at a fair price. And in the third situation, the buyer insisted on paying the major fraction of the price in cash.

Assets like property, art pieces by famous artists or even corporate fixed deposits which have a fixed tenure can be valuable; but are not always easy to convert into cash when you're in a pinch. The risk with them, therefore, is called **illiquidity.**

Imagine investing in a company that appears successful, only to later find out that it is actually faking its financials. Before long, your investment sums are likely to vanish. For example, in 2016, GainBitcoin became highly popular in India. The scheme promised 10 per cent monthly returns on Bitcoin investments and for two years, drew in thousands of investors. Come 2018, it unravelled and was found out to be a Ponzi scheme. The scale of the fiasco was estimated at an approximate ₹6,600 crores. Many investors could have avoided losing their money if they'd been vigilant and aware of the risk of **fraud**.

On another note, a friend of mine spent two years diligently saving for a trip to the States. She had calculated everything down to the last detail, confident that her savings were on track. Her investments grew by 6 per cent over three years, and she was excited to finally book her dream trip. But then inflation, which had quietly crept up higher than the rate of growth of her savings, threw the ultimate spanner in the works. The cost of her dream trip had risen by 50 per cent in three years! So despite her 6 per cent return, inflation had effectively reduced her purchasing power, leaving her short of what she needed for the trip. This is the harsh reality of **negative real returns**.

Investments are also exposed to the risk of fluctuations. Let's say you buy a stock at ₹100, which jumps to ₹120 in the next week. You get all excited about the quick profit you've just made. A week later, the stock comes down to ₹70. Now, you may end up worrying about this unexpected loss. However, it is important to remember that this loss is only on paper and won't impact you unless you try to sell this stock at this stage when its value is lower than what you bought it at. A good stock will typically recover from losses like this over a medium to long run; it may just be a matter of waiting patiently. Such fluctuations in your investments, however, are called **market risk** and are usually temporary.

Not all these risks apply to every type of investment. Just like each ride in the amusement park, different investment instruments come with their own combinations of risks and returns. There are, of course, strategies to reduce the impact of such events on your investments. In the upcoming chapters, we will delve into different kinds of investment classes and examine the risks and returns so that you can choose what's best for your life and your money.

How to Manage Risk

Just like in the aviation industry, there are checks to reduce risks while flying, there are ways to manage risks in investing as well. It doesn't mean they completely go away, but that you can reduce their impact on your money. For instance, many companies restrict how much of their senior management travels on one flight, so as to minimize the effects on its overall functioning in the rare, unfortunate event of a crash. Let's travel back in time to 2008. If all you had on your entire portfolio were equities, you'd be in for a not-so-pleasant surprise. The global recession would have chopped your portfolio by a whopping 52 per cent! But if you had spread your investments out, say by putting 60 per cent of your money in equities, 20 per cent in debt instruments and 20 per cent in gold, what do you think it might have done for your money? Here are the two options below:

Option 1

Asset	Returns in 2008 (%)	% of Portfolio
Equity	-52	60
Debt	8.80	20
Gold	16	20
Total Returns		-26%

Option 2

Asset	Returns in 2008 (%)	% of Portfolio
Equity	-52	100
Debt	8.80	0
Gold	16	0
Total Returns		-52%

As you can see, choosing Option 1 is clearly the smarter option: you have not put all your eggs in one basket. This strategy is called **diversification** and in

2008, it could have saved you much of your wealth by restricting your loss percentage to 24 per cent rather than 52 per cent when the recession came.

Besides diversification, another important consideration is being able to access your money when you need it. One of my uncles had been investing for his daughter's education since 2010 and did not have need for the money he was stowing away until 2020. By 2019, he had gathered up a corpus of ₹10 lakh. But just as he was about to pull the money out, the market crashed by 38 per cent due to the pandemic. His ₹10 lakh dropped to ₹6.2 lakh. A true disaster, right? Was there a way he might have been able to do better?

Enter **liquidity planning**. It would have been a smart move to shift his investments from equities to fixed income assets a year or two before his 2020 goal. This would have enabled him to keep his investments safe and less at the mercy of the market, and he'd have had access to the funds he needed whenever he wanted.

Finally, let's talk about the magic of **time**, which can be a powerful ally, especially during volatile times in the market. As mentioned before, in the long run, markets usually tend to bounce back from short-term dips, and by staying invested, you can ride these waves to enjoy greater positive returns. For example, if you put your money in the stock market and stick with it for ten to twenty years, you're likely to coast through the short-term highs and lows to see your investments grow steadily, as detailed in later chapters. Before we go deeper into the various asset classes, remember that good risk management is about maximizing your returns while limiting your losses.

> **KEY LEARNINGS**
>
> - Understand the kind of risk associated with the investment options you have.
> - Accept only that level of risk which you are comfortable with. Learn how to manage it.
> - Diversify your investments to minimize loss.
> - Stay invested for the long term as far as possible.

6

RETURNS

Good Enough Is Actually Great

Once, one of my favourite uncles once came over for a family lunch to our house. We went to great lengths to ensure his favourite dishes were cooked. He arrived in his usual fashion, making the same kind of jokes I'd enjoyed hearing since my childhood. When we finally settled around the table, my uncle, who had traditionally invested only in FDs, brought up a new topic of discussion.

'In other news,' he said, 'I've moved from barely earning 7 per cent returns on my FDs to a solid 14 per cent on mutual funds. And guess what? My financial goals are back on track!'

'That's great,' my father said matter-of-factly. 'I myself have been averaging 43 per cent returns for the last two years.'

My uncle's fork froze in midair. He was now staring at the paneer hanging precariously from its end, slipping down its spikes. It seemed he had suddenly lost his appetite and his face started drooping. I could see him mentally calculating all those missed gains, imagining all the riches that could have been his if he had got the same returns on his investments as my father. The cheery atmosphere had suddenly grown completely silent at the drop of a number.

'What? 43 per cent?!' My uncle said. 'I've been cheated!'

'One second, uncle,' I asked, 'is palak paneer better than gulab jamun?'

'*Arey beta*, how can you compare the two? They are different kinds of dishes.'

'Exactly,' I said. 'You are earning 13–14 per cent returns from a relatively less risky portfolio comprising hybrid and diversified equity mutual funds. Dad, on the other hand, has been investing in small-cap funds where the risks are high and so are the rewards. Comparing your portfolios is like comparing palak paneer to gulab jamun.'

I managed to reassure my uncle, but this is a fairly common sentiment among people. Many investors who earn meaningful absolute returns on instruments of their choosing and manage to meet their goals, suddenly feel a pang of dissatisfaction when they hear about someone else's gains. This incident reminded me of the movie *Three Idiots* (2009), where Farhan and Raju nervously approach the notice board displaying their semester results and scan the list for their names. Farhan's face falls as he sees his name near the bottom – he barely passed. Raju had also just about scraped by. But they don't find their friend Rancho's name anywhere in the vicinity and so deduce with great disappointment that he's failed. As they get caught up with worrying about him, they learn that Rancho had scored the highest in the exams. Rather than feeling happy for their friend, they are drowned in disappointment. Farhan sums it up perfectly when he says, '*Dost fail ho jaaye toh dukh hota hai, lekin dost first aa jaaye toh zyada dukh hota hai.* (It's upsetting if your friend fails, but it's even more upsetting if your friend ranks first.)'

Haven't we all seen parents comparing the achievements of their children to that of the neighbour's? Somehow, the achievements of *Sharma ji ka beta* (Mr Sharma's son) are always placed on the higher pedestal. But here's the thing: your investments should align with your personal financial goals, risk tolerance and time horizon – so there's no room to compete with your bragging neighbour. Beware of the Great Indian Sharma ji trap while investing!

Kitna Milega?

When you look into investing, the first question you'll probably feel like asking is '*kitna milega*?' or 'how much will I get in return for what I invest?' This question, while natural, is not the best place to start. The better question would be to ask, '*kitna chahiye*?' or 'what do I need to make this investment?'

Let's look at Karan, who wanted to buy a house – an aspiration he had in common with many in our country. He wanted to save ₹10 lakh for a down payment in five years. With the ₹7.5 lakh he already had saved, he was marching confidently towards his goal. Over a cup of chai, Karan shared his plan with his friend Neena, who made some quick calculations.

'To keep up with the 5 per cent annual inflation, you'll actually need around ₹12.7 lakh (₹10 lakh + ₹2.7 lakh due to inflation) in five years,' she said. 'And to reach that from ₹7.5 lakh,' she said, 'you'll need around 11.21 per cent annual returns.'

'How did you know that?' Karan asked.

Here's the calculation Neena had used for the required rate of returns:

> **Required returns = [(Future value adjusted for inflation / Current value) * (1/no. of years)] − 1**

Now they get to the fun part.

'So how much return do you need?' Neena asked.

'Around 12 per cent …' Karan answered.

'Yes, and such rates of returns can never be achieved through an FD or debt instruments. You will have to opt for a higher return-generating instrument, like equity or mutual funds. Now, how much time do you have?'

He had five years to reach his target. In that kind of time frame, he could afford to invest in equities and ride out the market's short-term fluctuations. If he had had less time to achieve his target, their strategy couldn't have worked. If you're wondering if equity can generate an average of 11–12 per cent annually for five years, the answer is a cautious yes.

Neena then asked, 'How much drama can you handle? It's a risky market in the day-to-day.'

Markets are naturally volatile, reacting to economic events and investor sentiment. But while in the short term, trends can be unpredictable, history has shown that markets generally rise over time. Neena made Karan understand fully that if he invested in high-return instruments, their value would fluctuate on a day-to-day basis. Some people have a high tolerance for such market risk. Some don't. Karan belonged to the first category.

'I think I can handle that,' he said.

'Great, because the idea of losing even 10 per cent of my capital gives me the shivers.'

The solution to Karan's problem was 12 per cent returns for five years, which could probably be achieved through equities or mutual funds, while also matching his risk appetite. Did he need to take more risk with his capital to earn 20 per cent returns? Given his goal, not really. In this scenario, Karan's expectations of the rate of returns and time horizon were realistic. But what if someone wants to double their money in a year? Well, then they need to revisit their goal because no financial instrument will provide those kinds of returns. And even if they do manage to find such a magic wand, it can get them into deep trouble, leaving them exposed to either extremely high market risks, or fraud.

You may be tempted to ask why we are saying 12 per cent returns are realistic whereas 30 per cent returns are not. Many investment apps show that some stocks or mutual funds have given 30–40 per cent returns in the last couple of years. But for every asset class, there is a realistic long-term return rate and a time horizon that is sensible to keep it invested for. For equities, this rate is 10–12 per cent. And why is this around the 12 per cent mark? The answer may seem difficult to find, but once you see it, you realize its simplicity: it is generally reflective of the rate at which the economy grows plus the rate of inflation. Here's how past realistic returns of some asset classes look:

Time Horizon	Asset Class	Average Returns (%)	Minimum Returns (%)	Risk of Earning Negative Returns in the Given Time Horizon
Up to 3 years	Debt	6.94	2.26	Low
	Equity	17.67	-9.02	High
	Gold	12.52	-9.95	High
Up to 5 years	Debt	7.20	3.22	Low
	Equity	16.66	-1.40	Moderate
	Gold	12.48	-2.98	Moderate
Up to 10 years	Debt	7.48	4.91	Low
	Equity	15.52	5.04	Low
	Gold	11.22	3.07	Low

The above figures are based on rolling returns of various asset classes from January 2005 to December 2024, with equity represented by the Nifty 500 TRI, debt by the CRISIL Composite Bond Index, and gold by LBMA AM INR rates. The data is sourced from ACE MF software. Past performance is not an indication of future performance.

Tip: A 100-metre sprinter and a marathon runner will have different strategies to win their races. Invest based on your time horizon.

Use Your Superpower

Time and again, we harp upon the importance of *time*. Why is it so critical? Because time is the superpower which unleashes the magic of compounding on your capital and makes it grow. Confused? Come, pour yourself a drink and I'll tell you a little story that goes perfectly well with it.

On a vacation in the beautiful country of Scotland, I visited a distillery. Its weathered walls were covered with ivy. A warm amber glow of light reflected off the copper stills and rows of oak barrels filling the air with the scent of malt and history. The keeper, a tall Scotsman with a thick accent and a twinkle in his eye, greeted me with a grin.

'Yer about to see how we take water, barley and a

touch o' magic,' he said in his Scottish accent, 'and turn it into the finest single malt you'll ever taste.'

He led me past the copper stills and stopped before a massive wooden cask. The malt takes only ten to fifteen days to make, he explained to me, but the true magic begins only after that. Once the malt is in the cask, it just sits there for *years*. Years and years. In fact, the beverage can't even be marketed as whiskey for the first three years. During this time, the brew endures all kinds of weather, absorbs the scents of the cask and grows more valuable with time.

The financial enthusiast in me plunged into the economics. 'How does the price change as the malt ages?'

He smiled knowingly. 'Take this twelve-year-old bottle,' he said, picking up a bottle worth £40. 'Let it age to eighteen years and it's £80.'

'Are you telling me it doubles in price in half the time?!'

'Yep. And that's not all! If you let it sit for twenty-three years, you'll be sitting on a £400 bottle, but if you hold onto it for just two more years, you can sell it at £2,000! That's a 4,900 per cent increase from its original price.'

'So the longer you wait, the more it's worth?'

'Exactly. With time, the value increases exponentially. Whiskey, like the best investments, needs time.'

As I left the distillery, the keeper's words echoed in my mind. Investing *is* a lot like ageing a fine whiskey, where time is the key ingredient to unlocking its most extraordinary value. In the initial years, returns might seem slow and incremental, much like the subtle flavour changes in a young whiskey. But as compounding takes effect, the value of investments begins to grow exponentially. Similarly, long-term investments can yield returns that are disproportionately larger than the initial gains. A comparison of the compounding effect on value of whiskey and a Nifty investment is tabularized below:

Age of Whiskey	Value (in £)
12 years	40
18 years	80
23 years	400
25 years	2,000

Age of Investment in Nifty 50 TRI	Value of `1 lakh today (in lakhs)
5 years	2.27
10 years	2.91
15 years	5.26
20 years	13.24
25 years	19.63

Data as on March 2025. Data Source: ACE MF. Past performance is not indication for future returns.

HOW COMPOUNDING WORKS

Imagine you invest ₹10,000 at an interest rate of 10 per cent per year. The interest is added to your current investment amount at the end of each year.

Time invested	Interest earned at 10 per cent (₹)	Investment amount at the end of year (₹)
1 year	1,000	11,000
2 years	1,100	12,100
3 years	1,210	13,310

As you can see, each year, you earn interest on the new total amount in your fund, which grows a lot faster over time. Thus, the longer you leave your money to grow, the bigger the compounded interest will be!

Remember, a good investment is like a strong relationship. It thrives when you have realistic expectations, the intent of tiding through the ups and downs by sticking together and giving it the time it needs to truly grow. Just as a relationship deepens with trust and commitment, your investments will flourish if you give them the attention and care they deserve.

KEY LEARNINGS

- Focus on what you need, not just what you want.
- Don't compare your returns with others' – it may be like comparing palak paneer with gulab jamun.
- Patience and time are your best allies.

7

TAXES

From CTC to Reality, Mind the Gap

Have you heard about the mango seller who managed to afford top-notch education for his children abroad?

In a village in Konkan, everyone bought Alphonso mangoes from Rajan because they were simply the best. Rajan was making decent money and lived modestly, but here's the kicker: his children were studying in prestigious institutions overseas! This left the other villagers puzzled and rumours of his ill-gotten gains soon reached the tax authorities.

A tax officer was sent to investigate Rajan's finances. To his surprise, all of Rajan's paperwork was in order and all his accounts were properly audited, no discrepancies could be found. Then what was the secret to Rajan's prosperity? Well, rather than seeing the tax system as a burden, he was able to use it to his advantage. He had invested wisely, leveraging deductions, credits and tax-free bonds to legally fund his lifestyle and afford to improve his children's prospects. In financial circles, Rajan was what you would call a 'tax whisperer'.

The moral of the story: Taxes aren't just something you have to pay (and later crib about). They're something you need to understand to be able to manage. For this, let's get the basics down.

Taxation in India

Mr Mehta was discussing his taxes with his wife when his teenage son chimed in with a question: 'Why do you pay taxes, dad?'

'Son, think of the government as the manager of our neighbourhood,' Mr Mehta answered. 'They build the roads, trains, airports and hospitals we use, and it all costs money to build and run. This money comes from our taxes.'

'And how do you pay them?'

'I get a salary, so my tax is deducted from my paycheck every month. It's called TDS, short for Tax Deducted at Source. If Dad bought you an ice cream every Sunday, but before handing it to you, took a small bite out of it every time, that would be TDS. It is taken out of your ice cream share before it reaches you. At the end of every year, I file an income tax return so any differences in the government's estimate of what I owe and my own calculations can be settled. Now imagine your friend Rohan buys his own ice cream, eats as much as he wants and then at the end, gives a bite to his parents because they asked for it. This is like him paying his taxes later – he gets to decide how much to give after he has had his fill. That's how your Sunita Maasi does it as the owner of a café, she calculates and declares her income to the government at the end of the year herself, and then pays her taxes directly.'

This difference in method of payment is because while an income from a job typically includes salary, bonuses, allowances and any other benefits provided by your employer, income earned from running your own business or profession – including profits from selling goods or services – as well as any income generated from business investments is classified as business income. Both attract direct taxes.

The child nodded slowly: direct taxes are straightforward – you earn or own something, and you pay a portion of it directly to the government. 'So what kind of direct taxes do people pay?' he asked.

'In India,' Mr Mehta explained, 'direct taxes come in a couple of flavours. **Income Tax** is the tax paid on the money you make. The rates for this are outlined every year in the Union Budget and vary with your income bracket.'

Wealth is measured through capital gains, among other means. Put simply, a capital asset is like a prized possession you've held onto – this could be property, stocks or even a rare painting. Capital gains are the profit you make when you sell that asset for more than what you bought it for. Such profit attracts a type of tax called the **Capital Gains Tax**. The rate of taxes you pay on an asset depends on how long you've owned it – short-term and long-term gains are taxed differently.

Current Capital Gains Tax Rates

As of the 2025 Union Budget, the tax rates and holding periods for various asset classes are as follows:

Asset Class	Period to Qualify as Long-Term Asset	Short-Term Capital Gains Tax Rate	Long-Term Capital Gains Tax Rate
Real Estate	24 months	Taxed at applicable slab rates	• For properties acquired before 23 July 2024: 20 per cent with indexation or 12.5 per cent without indexation. • For properties acquired on or after 23 July 2024: 12.5 per cent without indexation.
Domestic Equity and Equity-Oriented Mutual Funds	12 months	20 per cent	Gains up to ₹1.25 lakh exempt; balance taxable at 12.5 per cent.

Asset Class	Period to Qualify as Long-Term Asset	Short-Term Capital Gains Tax Rate	Long-Term Capital Gains Tax Rate
Debt Mutual Funds	24 months	Taxed at applicable slab rates	• For investments acquired prior to 1 April 2023: 12.5 per cent without indexation. • For investments acquired on or after 1 April 2023: Taxed at applicable slab rates.
Listed Bonds	12 months	Taxed at applicable slab rates	12.5 per cent
Fixed Deposits	Not Applicable	Interest income taxed at slab rates	Not Applicable
Gold	24 months	Taxed at applicable slab rates	12.5 per cent

Please note that tax laws are subject to change, and it is always advisable to consult with a tax professional or refer to official website of the Income Tax Department for the most current information.

'So dad,' the child said, 'if there are direct taxes, it means there would also be …'

'Indirect taxes,' Mr Mehta said, 'of course.'

Indirect Taxes are those which you pay as part of the price of something you are consuming, which are then passed on to the government. These include customs duty, charged on imports and collected by the central government, and the most comprehensive indirect tax in India, the Goods and Services Tax (GST).

Indirect taxes are what they are and not really in your control. With direct taxes, however, you can optimize how much you pay, as we will see in some examples in this chapter. With this lesson in the basics of the taxation system, Mr Mehta hoped that his child would go on to become not only a responsible tax-paying citizen, but also somebody who was aware of how to manage their taxes effectively within the ambit of the law – we will come back to their conversation to know how in a little while.

Tip: Tax planning today can mean more money in your pocket tomorrow.

Why Does Tax Matter?

Let's return to Rajan the mango seller–tax whisperer for a moment. He understood that ignoring tax norms would mean getting significantly less returns on his investments. Taxes could eat into his profits from interest, dividends and capital gains. Hence, he invested ₹10 lakh in stocks and after eleven months, when the value of his stocks grew to ₹12 lakh, he gauged if it was the right time to sell his stocks. Here is what his returns would have looked like at the time:

Scenario	Amount
Initial Investment	₹10 lakh
Sale Value After 11 months	₹12 lakh
Profit	₹2 lakh
Total Returns	20 per cent

However, in India, selling equity investments before one year makes the profit subject to Short-Term Capital Gains (STCG) Tax of 20 per cent. So if Rajan sold his stocks after 11 months, here's what his returns would look like after the tax deductions:

Scenario	Amount
Profit	₹2 lakh
Taxable Amount	₹2 lakh
STCG Tax (20 per cent)	₹40,000
Net Profit	₹1.6 lakh
Post-Tax Return	16 per cent

But the tax whisperer that he was, Rajan understood that waiting for just one more month would mean that he had held his stocks for a year and qualify him to pay the lower Long-Term Capital Gains (LTCG) tax on his investments, the rate for which is 12.5 per cent. Plus, the first ₹1.25 lakh of his gains would be tax-free (as is the norm). Thus, he would have to pay LTCG only on the remaining amount, resulting in a much higher return on his investments. The calculations would be as below:

Scenario	Amount
Profit (a)	₹2 lakh
Deduction from capital gains on which you need not pay any tax (b)	₹1.25 lakh
Taxable Amount (a) – (b)	₹0.75 lakh or ₹75,000
LTCG Tax (12.5 per cent)	₹9,375
Net Profit	₹1.91 lakh
Post-Tax Return	19.06 per cent

Rajan's understanding of the tax laws allowed him to save a portion of his profits. While the difference might seem small in case of this example, it can be significant in case of larger amounts. Over time, these gains can add up and significantly boost your returns. Hence, it is essential to understand taxation and optimize your returns.

How Do You Know Your Post-tax Returns?

Imagine you've been putting your money into an FD diligently for five years, enjoying a steady 7 per cent annual return. Sounds good, right? But here's the catch – since the returns on FDs are fully taxed according to your income tax slab, if you fall into the 30 per cent tax bracket, your post-tax return drops to just 4.9 per cent. Not as exciting anymore, is it?

Now what if you were open to taking a bit more

risk? Instead of sticking with the FD, you could invest in a **hybrid mutual fund** (we'll explain these asset classes in the upcoming chapters), which divides your money between equities (for growth) and debt (for stability). The best part? If you hold your investment for more than a year, the returns will be taxed at an LTCG rate of 12.5 per cent rather than 30 per cent. Plus, you'd have a better chance at earning better returns than a bank FD on your investments.

You can also save on capital gains tax by smartly selling your investments at the right time. A smart strategy is to sell just enough to use the ₹1.25 lakh LTCG exemption to your advantage. By doing this, you can gain ₹1.25 lakh in profits without paying any tax and then reinvest the money. For instance, if your total LTCG is ₹1.75 lakh, the first ₹1.25 lakh is tax-free, and only the extra ₹50,000 will be taxed at 12.5 per cent, leading to a ₹6,250 tax bill. This would be especially helpful for investments that have performed poorly or resulted in losses – you can sell those to preserve your gains. This could reduce or eliminate your total taxable income. For instance, if your losses match or exceed your taxable gains, you can reduce your tax liability to zero. This strategy allows you to manage taxes efficiently while maintaining your investment strategy.

TAX LOSS HARVESTING

Here's an example of how offsetting gains and losses works. Let's say you have the following capital gains and losses in a financial year:

LTCG on Equity Funds: ₹1.52 lakh

Long-Term Capital Loss (LTCL) from another Equity Fund: ₹50,000

Now, under the tax rules:

- The first ₹1.25 lakh of LTCG is tax-free. Hence, the taxable LTCG is ₹1.52 lakh – ₹1.25 lakh = **₹27,000**
- However, since you have a **long-term capital loss of ₹50,000**, you can use it to offset the taxable gain of ₹27,000.
- After offsetting, your **net taxable LTCG becomes ₹0**, meaning you don't have to pay any taxes on it.

If your **capital loss was higher** (say ₹80,000), the extra **₹53,000** (₹80,000 – ₹27,000) could be carried forward for future years to offset against LTCG in upcoming years, up to eight years. This strategy, also known as **tax-loss harvesting**, helps investors reduce or eliminate tax liability while staying invested in the market.

Efficient Tax Investing Strategies

Sneha had just landed a job at an aviation training company, and while she was thrilled about starting her career, her taxes were really bothering her. Frustrated, she decided to bring it up with one of her seniors at work during lunch.

'So much of my salary just goes into taxes!' she said, poking at her food angrily.

Her senior smiled, reminded of their own early career struggles. 'I used to feel the same way,' they said. 'But there are ways to lighten that load. Have you thought about opening a Public Provident Fund (PPF), Employee Provident Fund (EPF) or National Pension Scheme (NPS) account?'

Sneha looked puzzled. 'I've heard of them, but I don't really know how they work.'

The senior explained. Investing in PPF, EPF and NPS shrinks your taxable income, thanks to exemptions available under Section 80C.

Public Provident Fund or PPF is like a government-sponsored bank with a fifteen-year lock-in period. The interest and final payout are completely tax-free, making it a safe and tax-smart investment. Next, we have the Employees' Provident Fund or EPF, which is meant to serve as your retirement cushion as a salaried employee. Both you and your employer chip in, and as long as you follow some rules, the whole amount – including interest – can be withdrawn tax-free upon retirement. Finally, there's the National Pension Scheme or NPS, a flexible retirement plan that lets you invest in both stocks and bonds. It not only gives you tax breaks under Section 80C and 80CCD(1B), but also allows you to make partial withdrawals upon retirement without paying tax. So these investments not only grow your money in the long term, but also help you save big on taxes!

'Plus, the growth within these accounts is tax-deferred,' the senior said, 'which means you don't have to pay taxes on the earnings until you withdraw the money.'

Sneha's eyes widened a bit. 'Oh wow! Thanks for the tips!'

'No problem. Oh, by the way, if you're looking for something with a shorter lock-in period, consider Equity-Linked Saving Scheme or ELSS funds. These also qualify for deductions under Section 80C. They have a lock-in of just three years, which is shorter than most other tax-saving options.'

'Thank you! I'm going to look into these right away.'

The senior smiled. 'Great! If you treat tax like your friend, you'll soon learn to accept it and make the most of your finances!'

If it all still sounds like too much of a hassle to you, you can always switch over to the new tax regime. Under this, your income up to ₹12.75 lakhs is tax-free, and any taxes due are auto-calculated for your convenience.

Should Tax Be the Deciding Factor While Investing?

While taxes are definitely important, they certainly shouldn't be the star of the show when you're making investment decisions. Your real focus should be on finding investments that match your goals and risk threshold. After all, what's the point of a tax break if you're not getting any closer to what you really want?

Also, it is crucial to remember that **tax laws change**. Regularly check on your investments and be ready to make any adjustments if there is a change in tax regulations or your financial situation. By doing this, you can keep tax surprises at bay and make sure your financial strategy aligns with your goals. As a rule of thumb, between two investment instruments which provide equal returns, the tax-efficient choice is the better one.

KEY LEARNINGS

- Smart investors turn taxes from a burden into a tool for building wealth.
- The right timing can save substantial taxes.
- Tax efficiency is the silent driver of higher returns.

8

INSURANCE

The Parachute, Not the Plane

One evening, Ravi let out a scream and complained of a sharp pain in his chest. His wife Sangeeta comforted him saying it might just be a bit of indigestion – after all, he was only forty-two. But by midnight, they were in the emergency room, surrounded by beeping machines and doctors rushing around. It turned out that Ravi had a serious heart condition and needed immediate surgery.

Sangeeta was a schoolteacher and Ravi, an office admin. They lived a simple, happy life together with their two kids in Pune. Their days were filled with school runs, weekend picnics and the occasional movie. Life was sweet until this medical emergency showed up. The doctor's words hit her like a ton of bricks. Ravi needed a bypass surgery and the procedure costed about ₹5 lakhs, minimum. This included charges for pre-surgery tests, Intensive Care Unit stays and follow-up consultations.

Medical bills soon piled up – tests, scans, medications, consultations draining away their little savings. They had a few FDs, but all for small amounts, which they had to break prematurely, incurring penalties on their interest rates.

Left with no other options, Sangeeta had to sell off her gold jewellery to pay the hospital bills. Ravi eventually recovered, but their finances didn't. But what haunted Sangeeta most was her biggest nightmare nearly turning into her reality – losing her husband and raising their two kids by herself on a single income. She was quick to realize the importance of insurance. If they had health insurance, they could have covered Ravi's medical bills. And if, God forbid, Ravi hadn't survived, his life insurance would've been her lifeline, helping her manage on her own.

Here's a shocking fact – only around 4 per cent of Indians have adequate insurance. Compare that to 80 per cent of people living in countries like the US. Most of us don't even think about it until it's too late. You don't want your family's future to depend on good luck. It is better to make sure they're protected, come what may. The key takeaway is: *Sabse pehle* insurance, i.e. insurance above all.

Understanding Insurance and Its Purpose

After Ravi's health scare, Sangeeta wanted life insurance to secure their kids' future. But given Ravi's condition, it was now difficult for him to get either health or life insurance. So Sangeeta decided to at least insure herself. She met with Aditi, an insurance advisor to plan for her needs.

'In my current situation, I desperately need life insurance to ensure a safe future for my children – but where do I even start? Should I focus on high returns or a money-back policy?'

Aditi smiled. 'Insurance is about protection, not growing your money. When you buy insurance, you're buying a promise that if something unexpected happens, the insurer will shoulder the financial burden.'

'So ... it's not like an investment?'

'It is not. Investments are meant to grow your wealth, but insurance is focused on saving your money in unfortunate circumstances.'

'So what are my options?'

Aditi explained that **Term Life Insurance** offers pure insurance with low premiums and high coverage for a set period. A **premium** is the amount you pay for obtaining the benefits of the policy in the future. This can be paid monthly, quarterly or annually, depending on the nature of your policy. If the insured person loses their life during the validity period of their policy, their family receives the **sum assured** to cover expenses like debts, their living costs, etc. The sum assured is the guaranteed payout promised by the insurer in such events. Which in turn means no payout if nothing happens – which is why term insurance is more affordable.

'What about those plans in which you get your money back?'

'Those are **Endowment Plans**, which combine insurance and give you additional income as well. But their premiums are much higher and they offer lesser protection compared to term insurance.'

In endowment plans, part of the premium is allocated to life cover, while the rest is invested by the insurer. On **maturity** – the date on which the policy ends – if the policyholder has survived, they receive the sum assured plus bonuses or returns. If not, the beneficiaries they name get the sum assured.

'And what are "ULIPs"?' Sangeeta said.

'Unit-Linked Insurance Plans, or ULIPs, combine insurance with investments that are market-linked.'

ULIP premiums are split between insurance cover and investment in market-linked funds. The insurer will invest the money you pay them in premiums in equity market-linked products, such as large-cap or mid-cap stocks, or bonds. The value of your investment depends on the market performance of the chosen funds. ULIPs have a lock-in period and are more suited for those looking for both insurance and long-term investment growth.

Sangeeta was now clear on the fact that the fundamental purpose of insurance was to cover risks, not to generate returns. If it is market-linked investing you're looking for, however, there are better options available like mutual funds, stocks, bonds and retirement accounts, which we will talk about in more detail in later chapters. For this reason, mixing insurance with investments usually results in lower coverage and higher costs.

After hearing all of this, Sangeeta felt more confident to make a choice that met *her* needs. 'I'm ready to go ahead with a term insurance plan,' she declared.

Tip: Buying term plans is cheap, skipping them is costly.

How Much Life Insurance Cover Is Enough?

It would have been beneficial for Sangeeta's family to have made this decision regarding insurance earlier for Ravi as well, while he was still healthy. They were now forced to make a decision under pressure. But you must be wondering how a middle-class family is supposed to plan for insurance during calmer times? With two kids, a modest apartment and dreams of home ownership, how can they know what insurance plan is right for them? How much cover do they need?

A simple formula for this is:

> Insurance Needed = (Annual Expenses + Inflation) × Years to Support Family + Liabilities + Major Expenses

To determine the right life insurance coverage for you, start by calculating your monthly expenses. Suppose your current monthly expenses are around ₹50,000. This means your annual expenditure is about ₹6 lakhs, which is the minimum amount your family will need in a year to maintain their standard of living in your absence.

Next, adjust this amount for inflation and investment returns. Assuming an inflation rate of 5 per cent/year and an expected return of 7 per cent/year on the insurance payout, the net return is approximately 2 per cent/year. If you anticipate that your family may need financial support for the next thirty years, you can use the **Present Value of Annuity formula** to estimate the required corpus. By applying this calculation, the amount needed to sustain these annual expenses over thirty years is approximately ₹1.28 crore.

Beyond covering daily expenses, it is important to factor in any outstanding liabilities. If you have a home loan of ₹30 lakhs and a car loan of ₹5 lakhs to pay off, you should include these sums in your calculation to ensure that your family is not burdened with debt after you. Additionally, you must also plan for future financial commitments. If you anticipate spending ₹20 lakhs on your children's education and ₹10 lakhs on their weddings, these costs should be added to the total insurance requirement as well.

Summing up all these components – ₹1.28 crores for household expenses, ₹35 lakhs for outstanding loans, and ₹30 lakhs for future financial commitments – the total recommended life insurance coverage would come to ₹1.93 crores. By securing this amount, you ensure that your family can continue to live comfortably, free from financial worries, even in your absence.

You can download the insurance calculator excel sheet from the Mango Millionaire website.

Checklist

- ☐ **Coverage:** Can the policy fully cover your family's financial needs, outstanding loans and future expenses?
- ☐ **Exclusions:** What are the exclusions? Any mention of risky professions, hobbies, or activities that might affect your claim?
- ☐ **Waiting Period:** Are there any restrictions on claims within the first few years of the policy?
- ☐ **Premium Affordability:** Can you pay the premium amount consistently without feeling financial strain?
- ☐ **Claim Settlement:** Does your insurer have a high claim settlement ratio to ensure a hassle-free experience?
- ☐ **Read the Fine Print:** Did you take the time to review the details before signing up? This isn't something you want to overlook.

Health Insurance: Shielding Your Savings from Medical Emergencies

Rahul was buzzing with excitement after landing a new job at a digital marketing agency. As he skimmed through his offer letter, one thing jumped out at him: health insurance. The employer was deducting a certain fraction of his annual salary towards an insurance premium. Sitting at a café with his friend Akash, an insurance professional, Rahul decided to bring it up.

'I don't get it – why do I need this now?' he asked, stirring his coffee. 'I'm young and healthy.'

'Everyone thinks that way until the unexpected happens,' Akash said. 'Health insurance isn't just for emergencies. In some cases, it covers routine checkups too, saving you considerable money. And don't forget to check if your parents are covered in your policy too.'

'The company covers me and they have given me the option to include my parents as my dependents as part of my policy.'

'What's the coverage like?'

'About ₹3 lakh.'

'That's a good start, sure, but basic coverage won't always cut it. Your father is pre-diabetic – if you change jobs and your new company doesn't offer group insurance the same way, you could be exposed to the risk of running really high medical bills if his condition turns chronic.'

'So how much health insurance should I plan for?'

'Depends on your personal situation, where you stay and the cost of the medical facilities around you. Considering all this in your particular situation, I would say about ₹15–20 lakhs coverage should be good. The cost of good healthcare is also constantly rising.'

'What are my options then?'

Akash explained that while **individual health insurance** covers just you, a **family floater insurance** shares coverage among immediate family members. It covers medical expenses for illnesses, accidents, surgeries, hospitalization, day-care procedures, etc.

'What if someone develops a serious health condition?'

'For serious illnesses like cancer, a **critical illness insurance** would give you a lump sum payout upon diagnosis. You get a fixed amount upfront for treatment, lifestyle changes, or replacing lost income.'

'Can we get more insurance cover if our coverage runs out due to high medical expenses in a given year?'

'Well, you can get a **top-up health insurance** for such scenarios.'

A top-up insurance plan offers extra coverage beyond your basic health insurance, but it kicks in only after you've used up a certain amount, known as the **deductible**. For example, if your regular plan covers ₹3 lakhs, a top-up with a ₹3 lakh deductible would start paying only after that sum is exhausted. **Super top-up plans** enhance your health insurance by covering multiple claims throughout the year once the deductible is met – unlike the regular top-up plans which cover only one claim after surpassing the set threshold. Super top-up plans consider the total medical expenses during the policy year, rather than a single claim.

'And what if I stay healthy all this time?' Rahul said.

'Then you are rewarded with a no-claim bonus!'

Many health plans offer a No-Claim Bonus or NCB for claim-free years by increasing your coverage without raising your premiums. The longer you remain claim-free, the higher the bonus, with some insurers offering 5–50 per cent, or even more. With all this in mind, here's a simple checklist of what you should verify while buying health and life insurance:

Checklist

- ☐ **Coverage:** Does your policy cover only hospital stays? What about pre- and post-hospitalization expenses?
- ☐ **Exclusions:** What expenses are not covered? Are your preferred hospitals part of the insurer's cashless network?
- ☐ **Waiting Period:** If you have pre-existing conditions, what is the specified waiting period? It typically ranges between one to four years.
- ☐ **Affordability:** What's your co-pay balance? Higher co-pay lowers premiums, but increases out-of-pocket expenses.
- ☐ **Claim Settlement:** Does your insurer have a high claim settlement ratio?

- ☐ **Read the Fine Print:** Have you read and understood all terms properly? Don't just click 'Agree' as if you were installing new software.

Avoiding Hard Sales Tactics

I was reviewing my aunt's finances after my uncle passed away and I noticed that nearly ₹30,000 were consistently being deducted every month. Curious, I asked, 'What's this outgo for?'

'Your uncle had invested this money for me,' she answered.

I asked to check the policy documents. *There we go.* I realized someone had sweet-talked him into buying a product that sounded like an investment. But surprise, surprise – it was an insurance–investment combo deal. Many middle-class families get caught up in schemes like these, locking away their savings in long-term plans. We even encountered a retiree with ₹1 crore in his PF, once, who had unknowingly invested it in insurance after confusing it for an investment. The key takeaway here is that insurance is *essential*, but so is getting the right kind and the right coverage, bought for the right reasons.

Buy what you need, not what's sold to you.

> **KEY LEARNINGS**
>
> - Health insurance ensures your treatment decisions aren't driven by your bank balance.
> - Keep protection and wealth creation separate. Always.
> - Read the fine print.

Resources

- Mango Millionaire website. Available at: https://mangomillionaire.in/.

PART II

THE BUILDING BLOCKS

9

REAL ESTATE

Buy a Home, Not the Hype

'*Aaj mere paas bungla hai* ... (Today, I have a bungalow ...)'

Amitabh Bachchan's line from *Deewaar* (1975) still hits home. It's from a legendary scene in the film where two brothers meet after their paths completely diverged from one another. Vijay, played by Bachchan, had to hustle hard to get from rags to riches, although his methods were questionable. Standing in front of the slum they grew up in, he proudly shows off his success to his brother: bungalow, car, bank balance.

The way he lists out his assets is in a certain peculiar order – Salim-Javed's dialogue was a true reflection of the popular sentiment that a '*bungla*' was the ultimate symbol of success. It's what so many Indians continue to aspire to – the dream of owning a big home. And if you managed to achieve it, it is treated as a tangible sign of you having *made* it in life.

But why is owning a home such a big deal? Well, there's some history to take into account here. After Independence, most people didn't own any land. Wealth was concentrated in a few hands owing to our age-old social systems of *zamindari*, and everyone else was left aspiring to it. So when people started earning a living, a house of their own became the ultimate status symbol for the Indian middle class. And as people started building their dream homes, movies reflected this change too. The evil *zamindars* (landlords) of Bollywood were swapped out for modern evils like rising EMIs, loans and inflation.

Khosla Ka Ghosla (2006) is a great example of this. It is a commentary on the middle-class obsession with owning land and the crazy lengths they'll go to protect that dream. Kamal Kishore Khosla, your average Delhiite, just wants to own a piece of land. But right when he thinks he's made it, a sneaky land shark named Khurana swoops in and snatches it away. What follows is a hilarious rollercoaster as the Khosla family tries every trick in the book to save the plot. These stories have shaped entire generations and home-owning remains the ultimate symbol of security and stability. It became an unspoken rule: buy your own house so no one can ever take that away from you, no matter how tough the going gets. But in modern-day India, the big question is: should you buy or just rent?

Buy or Rent?: The Perpetual Dilemma

Arjun and Karthik, two college friends from Bengaluru, had just started their first jobs at top IT companies. With their first paychecks in hand, they were eager to explore their newfound independence. Lattes in air-conditioned cafes replaced cutting chais and they ordered their meals from top restaurants over food delivery apps instead of eating at their hostel mess. Every weekend felt like an adventure and before long, they began thinking about their future.

'No more sharing cramped rooms, man,' Arjun said. 'I think I'm going to buy a flat.'

Karthik was surprised. 'We've barely just started working! How will you manage that?'

'There's this new project in a developing suburb close by. I'm planning to take a home loan and use my savings for the down payment. No more arguing with landlords refusing to let to bachelors.'

Karthik shook his head in disapproval. 'But have you even thought about the EMIs, maintenance and interest rates? How will you pay for all that?'

'It's an investment, bro, and property values only go up.'

'Yeah, I'm just going to rent a place closer to the office,' Karthik said. 'Less hassle and I can rack up some savings. Plus, I want the freedom to move around and travel if I want to.'

'Bro, renting is just like paying for your landlord's home loan!'

'Well, I'd rather spend on rent and not get tied down by a house for now. It gives me greater flexibility to just go wherever my job takes me.'

Fast forward to a year later, the two were sitting at the same café. Arjun was stressed out and busy juggling his finances to keep up with hefty EMIs towards his flat, while Karthik was enjoying his shorter commute and growing savings. Arjun couldn't remember the last time he went out for a movie or took a vacation – all his money was going towards his EMIs.

Karthik comforted his friend, 'That's tough, man, but hey, you have your own place now!'

Five years later, they met at a reunion again. Arjun told his friend that although the flat had once felt like a burden, but it seemed like a pretty solid investment now. He'd got engaged and his fiancée was happy they'd be living in a house that was soon going to be their own when they got married.

'I missed out on a lot because of the stress,' Arjun admitted. 'But the flat's value has gone up and now it's like having a security blanket around you at all times.'

Karthik, who had accumulated some savings, was now considering buying a home. Every few years, he had to move or pay higher rent every time his lease was renewed. Property prices had also risen from the time Arjun had purchased his house, which meant Karthik was looking at purchasing at a higher price. However,

Karthik was also feeling unsure about committing to a long-term mortgage and so was struggling to make a decision.

'Guess there's no perfect choice,' he said. 'It's all about what you value more – stability or freedom.'

'I think there's merit to both sides, my friend,' Arjun said.

So as you may have guessed by now, there is no one right answer to the rent-versus-buy debate. It is entirely personal. You could be like Arjun, valuing the security of owning a home over all else, or like Karthik, valuing the flexibility to move and invest. The key is to choose what aligns best with your values, goals and life stage. There's no one-size-fits-all solution and both paths have their own set of challenges and rewards.

The most important thing is to make an informed decision – knowing what you're willing to trade off and what matters most to you in the long run. After all, a house is more than just an investment – it's a crucial step in building a life of your dreams.

Calculating if You Can Afford a Home

As you would have observed in Arjun's situation, buying a home – especially early on in your career – can be a significant financial challenge due to the high EMIs and limited savings. Thus it is generally advisable to consider purchasing property once you have a solid savings pool to make a down payment. You can also follow the 30-

30-3 rule to ensure your home loan remains manageable:
- Save up to **30** per cent of the home's value before you buy. This will give you a head start – it'll make your EMIs lighter on your pockets and your lenders happier.
- Keep your EMI below **30** per cent of your monthly income. This way, you will not be living paycheck to paycheck and you can still enjoy your weekend outings. Never opt for an EMI so high that it gives you sleepless nights in the air-conditioned bedroom of your overly expensive dream home.
- Pick a property that costs no more than three times (**3x**) your annual income. This is a smart way to keep your budget in check and avoid drowning in debt.

Buying your first home also tends to be an emotional call rather than a financial one. In that sense, it differs from other traditional investment decisions. To have a roof of one's over their head can bring them peace of mind. Children cannot be raised under a financial spreadsheet and owning the home they grow up in can give them the invaluable lifelong sense of security and belonging as well.

In our observation over the years, Gen X and Y tend to be more inclined towards buying a home, while Gen Z and beyond seem to prefer to rent living spaces and not get tied down to a location or long-term financial commitment.

But what after you've purchased your first home? Should you buy more real estate as investment?

Tip: Renting isn't a waste and buying isn't always wise. The right choice depends on your individual lifestyle and financial condition.

Balancing Pride with Prudence

One Sunday morning, our family group chat was buzzing with the usual updates, when one of my cousins dropped a few photos: he'd just bought another house. Instantly, the chat exploded with congratulations. Everyone started praising him as if he'd just scaled Mount Everest. Meanwhile, another cousin, who often asks me for investment advice, had quietly made a substantial addition to his mutual fund portfolio. He made no public announcement of this fact. And even if he had, it would typically be considered inappropriate to flaunt such an investment, because how can you really show off a mutual fund?

In my view, buying a second home is more a decision governed by math than heart. When making such a purchase, real estate has to be evaluated against the same criteria as other investments. It comes with its own risks, just like any other instrument, and you should be aware of those. Some of these may include:

- **Illegal Constructions and Project Delays:** These are an unfortunate reality of the real estate industry. A recent example in Delhi was the illegal construction of two forty-storey towers, Apex and Ceyane, in Noida. These towers were built by Supertech Ltd and violated building norms, exceeding height limits and encroaching on space meant for green cover. In August 2021, the Supreme Court ordered the demolition of these towers, citing illegal approvals and collusion with Noida Authority officials. The towers were demolished in August 2022 and the video went viral on social media, setting a precedent for strict enforcement of building regulations and much-needed accountability in the sector. However, not all delays are illegal or unjustifiable. There are legitimate channels through which builders can request to push the possession date if there are unavoidable delays. The Real Estate Regulatory Authority (RERA) outlines the procedures to do so legally.
- **Moderate Gains:** People tend to take pride in the value of their property rising. Once, one of my friends proudly announced, '*ek ka do ho gaya*', meaning the ₹1 crore property they had invested in was now worth ₹2 crores. However, he was not doing the entire math. I asked him to factor in how much interest had been paid on his loan for purchasing the property, the principal outstanding, and in how much time the

property value had doubled. If we just take the price appreciation of the property in the thirteen years that he had held it and convert it into Compound Annual Growth Rate (CAGR), it works out to a mere 5.5 per cent. When we add the interest he paid and other costs of maintenance of the property, the CAGR dropped to a mere 4.2 per cent.

It is important to remember that the price appreciation of a property depends (amongst other factors) on the location, upcoming development projects and how saturated the property prices are in the area. But in general, property prices tend to double in about twelve to fourteen years. Compare that to a regular FD, which will double in ten years at 7 per cent rate of compounding. And compare that to a mutual fund which grows at 12 per cent each year – your investment can double in six years.

- **Invisible Fluctuations:** Some people treat real estate as a 'stable' investment compared to say, a mutual fund or stocks This perception has gained popularity because real estate investment are not monitored or evaluated every day like mutual funds or stocks would be. If property prices were to be listed and monitored on an index, it will also show fluctuations and periods of no growth, same as other investment instruments.
- **Illiquidity:** Another aspect to consider is the illiquidity of a real estate investment. One of my uncles, who had retired from his job, had invested in real estate

which was worth more than ₹1 crore. But there came a point where he needed ₹20 lakhs for another investment. Now there was no way he could partially liquidate a real estate investment, could he? This is the typical scenario of 'asset rich but cash poor'. You cannot sell a balcony or a bedroom of a flat if you need partial liquidity from your asset.

- **Rental Yield Considerations:** Many people buy real estate with the assumption that rent will provide them with a steady stream of passive income. However, the reality is that rental yields in India tend to be quite low. The rental yield, which is the annual rental income as a percentage of the property's market value, usually hovers between 2–3 per cent in residential real estate. Compare this to the dividend yields from equity investments or interest income from fixed deposits, which can often be higher. Additionally, rental income is subject to periods of vacancy, maintenance costs, property taxes and tenant-related risks, all of which can further eat into your returns.

There are two types of real estate: one for living and one for investing. Before buying property, figure out what you need it for and see if it aligns with your goals. Think it through!

KEY LEARNINGS

- A house is a home first and an investment second.
- A second home isn't a golden goose. Taxes, slow appreciation and zero liquidity can make it a bad bet. Do the math before you invest!
- Renting can provide freedom from EMIs and maintenance and allow greater flexibility.

10

GOLD

From Trousseau to Treasury

On my wedding day, I wore a beautiful Rani Haar, a kind of long, elaborate necklace that is often donned by brides in India. Beyond being embellished with gold, precious stones and pearls, it was meant to symbolize the years of my parents' hard work and their life's savings. Running my hands over its intricate patterns, I could feel the love which had been poured into it. Even before I was born, my parents used to purchase small amounts of gold as security, and when they had a daughter, they doubled down on their purchases. They'd wait for any occasion or any other excuse to buy gold – my birthdays, Diwali, and whenever gold prices fell.

I often questioned why. In my teenage years, my mother would often say, '*Beti ki shaadi ke liye* 10 *tola jama karna hai*', which meant that she wanted to gift me at least ten tolas of gold on my wedding day. Most Indian families have a figure like that in their mind for the amount of gold they want to gift to their daughters or daughters-in-law. A tola is a traditional Indian measure of weight for measuring precious items such as gold and is still widely used in that context. One tola of gold is equivalent to 11.66 grams, but is usually rounded off to 10 grams in India.

When I eventually started working in financial services, I remember asking my parents, 'Why gold? Wouldn't mutual funds or real estate have been more sensible investments all these years?'

But mother would just smile and say, 'This is more than money, Radhika. One day, you'll understand.'

At the time, I didn't get it. But fast forward to my own wedding, and it all suddenly made sense. Prices of gold had risen considerably since my first birthday. But thanks to the prudence of my parents, they had accumulated enough for my wedding jewellery through gold like an SIP, well before the term became as well-known.

That's when I realized gold wasn't just meant to provide financial security – it also inspired a sense of emotional security, which explains its immense popularity.

Why Is Gold Valuable?

When buying gold, my father would often say '*bhaav badh jayega*', meaning the price would eventually increase over time. And boy, was he right! In 1983, the price of 10 g of 24 karat gold was ₹1,800. Now it is nearly ₹90,000, as of March 2025. Rising by over 11.5 per cent CAGR during this period. Hence, gold is a good asset to add to your investment portfolio – but in the right proportion.

Gold cushions your investments through major economic downturns. Since it is priced in US dollars, when the Indian rupee weakens, gold becomes more valuable. Conversely, if the rupee strengthens, gold prices in the country fall even if global gold prices stay the same. Whenever the economy goes haywire – whether due to a stock market crash, a recession, or even a global crisis – gold generally retains its value. Lastly, gold is a rare commodity. Its scarcity imbues it with serious power, making it way less likely to lose value over longer term periods like ten to fifteen years, as compared to other assets.

On an individual level, this last bit is what prompts people to buy gold – it is treated as an umbrella of safety for rainy days. In many Bollywood movies, wives are shown to lease or sell their most beloved pieces of jewellery – even their precious *mangalsutras* – to save their husbands or families from financial distress. Gold is the commodity of choice amongst Indian women – can you guess how much of this shiny metal they own? As per unofficial estimates, the total value of gold held by women in India is equivalent to about 20 per cent of India's GDP! On the other hand, the Reserve Bank of India's gold reserves are said to be worth more than

$700+ billion. This means Indian women own more gold than the gold held by the RBI! Yeah – how's that for girl power?

Is Gold a Good Investment?

Gold has pulled off giving an impressive annual return rate of 11.5 per cent since 2000 – which is pretty solid! But there have been some bumps along the way. Some years, gold even dipped into the red or went totally flat for two to three years, offering zero returns. For example, between 2013–15, gold prices dropped consistently, from a peak of around ₹31,050 per 10 g in 2012 to ₹26,343 per 10 g by 2015. In this period, gold prices fell because the US dollar became stronger, interest rates went up and the global economy improved, making gold less appealing to investors.

So while the long-term gains look great, it hasn't been smooth sailing all the way. And like any other investment, gold also comes with its own advantages and disadvantages. Some of these are as below.

Why Gold?

- ✓ **Safety:** It is a reliable long-term investment.
- ✓ **Liquidity:** Easily sold at jewellers in emergency situations.
- ✓ **Returns:** It offers an impressive 11.5 per cent average since 2000.

- ✓ **Collateral:** It can be used as guarantee against short-term loans.

Why Not Gold?

- ✗ **No Regular Income:** You earn no dividends or interest on gold.
- ✗ **Volatility:** Its value can fluctuate majorly, and these changes often go unnoticed.
- ✗ **Storage Costs:** You need to invest in secure storage for it.
- ✗ **Short-term Risks:** There is a possibility of getting negative returns on your investment in the short term.

Tip: Gold in your portfolio is like salt in food. Essential, but can be overwhelming in the wrong proportion.

How Should You Invest in Gold?

Given how gold has always been considered a symbol of wealth and security, especially in India, there is no doubt about its reliability as a hedge. While it may not always offer the highest returns, it can shield you from market volatility and inflation in the long term. Many people often ask me how they can start investing in gold. Here's a list of the main options available:

- **Coins, Bars or Jewellery:** This is the classic route to investing in gold. If you sell gold after two years, expect to pay 12.5 per cent LTCG tax. In case of jewellery, you've got to factor in the making (or breaking) charges, which can eat into your returns. You'll also need to ensure its safe storage by paying for bank lockers, etc. Gold jewellery also acquires emotional value, and people generally grow hesitant to sell it, defeating its purpose as an investment. So if you want to *invest* in gold (and not just buy jewellery to wear), our advice would be to buy it through the other financial instruments below.
- **Gold ETFs (Exchange-Traded Funds):** A gold ETF (we'll talk about these in more detail in chapter 13) is bit a like a mutual fund in that it is traded on stock exchanges, so you can buy or sell whenever you want. All you need to have is a demat and broking account. They offer a high level of liquidity and there is no need for you to worry about bank lockers or security since everything's digital. The returns on these are linked to the prices of gold.
- **Sovereign Gold Bonds (SGBs):** These are issued by the Government of India and offer gold price appreciation plus a fixed 2.5 per cent annual interest. They have an eight-year maturity, but you can cash them out after five years if you need to. SGBs aren't as easy to trade as ETFs or gold funds but they're

tax-exempt on capital gains if you hold them till maturity, although they are no longer issued. Only the ones issued earlier are can still be traded on exchange and are available for traders to purchase. Just note that the interest you earn is taxable and selling early might mean lower liquidity and a dip in value.

- **Digital Gold:** This option lets you buy small amounts of gold online, making it convenient for those looking to invest in gold with a small budget without the hassle of safety and storage. However, lack of regulatory guardrails and transparency make it less reliable. It is also taxed like physical gold, and GST applies when you buy, making it a bit less tax-efficient than Gold ETFs or bonds.

While Indians have turned to gold as a means to guard their wealth and peace of mind for generations, it is wise to step back and weigh your options before you take the plunge. It won't make you rich like stocks might, but its value as a safety net is indisputable, especially when the markets mimic stormy seas.

Can your portfolio have 5–10 per cent of gold? Absolutely! 50 per cent? Probably not. It is best to use gold as a complementary asset, not as the centrepiece of your investment strategy.

KEY LEARNINGS

- Your mom's gold-buying habit is an SIP in safety. Yep, she had a strategy all along!
- Gold ETFs save you the headache of investing in a bank locker. Same investment, no storage hassles!
- Like you wouldn't put half your wealth into insurance, don't do so with gold either.

11

FIXED INCOME

A Sensible Sidekick

As a kid, I have vivid memories of my Tauji talking about a place called *dak khana*. If you were born in the '90s or later, you might be wondering what a dak khana even is. Well, it is the Hindi term for a 'post office' – a kind of place that used to be quite popular for a variety of functions in a world where emails did not exist. Ah, the days of the old wooden counters, postal stamps and red letter boxes!

Tauji visited the post office routinely every few months, either to deposit his savings or withdraw some cash. It was the go-to spot for traditional savings schemes like NSCs and Kisan Vikas Patras. Believe it or not, many of these schemes offered a guaranteed 11 per cent return back then. Yep, you heard that right. 11 per cent!

Interest rates used to be much higher back then than what they are today and people loved those guaranteed

11 per cent returns. While these schemes still exist, today's post office schemes offer around 7.7 per cent and yet, their charm persists. Tauji and millions of others continue to trust these products for one crucial reason: security.

No matter how the market conditions changed, their money grew steadily. For them and many other Indians, fixed-income products are like the old dak khana itself: reliable and comforting. But what exactly are fixed-income products? And why are they crucial for your portfolio?

What Are Fixed-Income Products?

Think of fixed-income products as a way to earn income by lending your money. Depending on whether you lend it to the government, corporate groups or banks, they would be called government securities, corporate bonds or fixed deposits, respectively. They could be called by any name, but as Shakespeare said, 'A rose by any other name would smell as sweet.'

All fixed-income products do the same thing: pay you steady interest, and when the term's up, your investment returns safe and sound – no surprises; just reliable returns. Let's look at the various fixed income product options and compare them to equity-like products (detailed in the next chapter) through the story of three superheroes – the Wizard of Wealth, Captain Stable and Captain Adventure who lived in the galaxy of Investara.

The Chronicles of Investara

One day, the Wizard of Wealth was approached by Captain Stable, an amazing, reliable, steadfast guy he could trust with his life.

'Oh, mighty Wizard of Wealth,' he said, 'I need 1,00,000 coins for a mission. I promise I'll repay you in full in two years – in fact, I'll even pay 7 per cent interest on it. Please, will you think about it?'

The wizard could feel the quiet allure of this offer. He was tempted to lend to Captain Stable as he was widely known to repay his debts on time. It felt safe. He was like a fixed-income product. But before the wizard could say yes, Captain Adventure burst onto the scene. Always seeking new thrills, Captain Adventure truly embodied his name.

'Wait, oh wealthy Wizard, I have a better proposal,' Captain Adventure said, his voice full of energy. 'I also need 1,00,000 coins for my gemstones business. There's no way my venture doesn't take off and when it does, I'll pay you back. Get this: I won't just return your entire loaned amount, but also include a good share of the profits I make – probably even more than Captain Stable's measly 7 per cent interest. So what do you say?'

The Wizard of Wealth felt the rush of excitement from Captain Adventure's words. He was like equities – glowing with the promise of high returns but also carrying high risk. But the sheer potential was exhilarating: immense rewards awaited him if this business venture soared – or great losses if it fell flat. Tempting, but did the wizard have the risk appetite such a decision demanded?

The Wizard of Wealth pondered over the two offers. In the end, he realized that each option had its own pros. Captain Stable's plan offered capital preservation, lower risk and steady returns. Captain Adventure's plan provided higher returns at the cost of a certain risk to the capital. So who should he lend to?

If you were the Wizard of Wealth, what would you do? Offer the 1,00,000 coins to Captain Stable (fixed-income products) or Captain Adventure (equities)? Well, while the answer will differ from person to person, a good overall strategy would be to allocate a certain percentage of your funds to both Captain Stable and Captain Adventure, respecting your own preferences for stability and adventure.

Role of Fixed Income in Your Portfolio

Remember my Tauji, who'd make regular trips to the post office for those sweet 11 per cent returns? Now that fixed-income products offer around 7 per cent, you might wonder, 'Are they even worth it when stocks can offer more?'

Here's the thing – stocks can be quite a ride, especially if crashes like 2008 recur. I would know! In 2007, when markets were doing well and I was an analyst on Wall Street, I had invested all my capital into equities. A year later, in May 2009, I decided to return to India to start my own venture, Forefront Capital Management, and needed capital to fund the venture. I was forced to withdraw my equity investments since they were all I had and the markets had tanked by 30–40 per cent. If I'd allocated a portion of my capital to fixed income products, however, I would not have lost my capital. That's why fixed-income products matter, especially for short-term goals and conservative investors. They provide stability without the roller-coaster risky ride of the stock market.

Risk and Returns in Fixed-Income Products

Let's go back to the galaxy of Investara, where the Wizard of Wealth was still considering the two offers from Captain Stable and Captain Adventure. Just as he was weighing how many of his precious coins to entrust to each captain, another character appeared in his chamber: Captain Credit Risk. He also wanted to start a business and had a proposal for the wizard.

'Wizard!' Captain Credit Risk said, 'Why settle for a mere 7 per cent interest from Captain Stable when I can offer you 10, or maybe even 11 per cent interest? Guaranteed! Think of the massive payback from leaving your prized coins with me!'

The wizard felt the pull, of course – who wouldn't? After all, *guaranteed* 11 per cent was considerably more than 7 per cent. But wealth was his area of expertise, and his wisdom steadied him. *What's going on here?* He recalled tales from the distant land of India, where the banking system, regulated by its government and the reserve bank had been carefully built on stable foundations and banks offered only safe returns of around 7 per cent on fixed-income investments. This was his benchmark of reliability and low risk.

Captain Credit Risk's offer was well above that benchmark, but he also had a shady history of not paying his dues on time. The Wizard of Wealth knew from experience that when someone promised such high guaranteed returns, there was often a catch. 'So, Captain Credit Risk, what's the story behind this extra interest you're offering? How did you manage 11 per cent?'

Captain Credit Risk chuckled. 'Ah, ever the wise wizard,' he said. 'To be honest, I'm working on a few ambitious missions on the downlow that need a bit of extra funding, and ... well ... let's just say the banks don't really want to back them. So I thought I'd offer you a chance to earn higher interest in return for showing a bit of ... trust.'

The wizard's eyes narrowed as he thought about **credit risk**, or the possibility that an investor might not get paid back if the borrower ran into trouble. Unlike Captain Stable, who had solid ground to stand on, Captain Credit Risk's ventures seemed more suspicious and unpredictable, and his ability to repay wasn't as certain. What if his missions didn't go as planned? The Wizard of Wealth could end up losing some or all of his coins. After all, the more uncertain a borrower's ability to repay, the higher the promised returns would need to be to attract investors. While the promise of 11 per cent shone brightly, the Wizard of Wealth decided to heed to Captain Credit Risk's poor track record.

'Captain Credit Risk,' the wizard said, 'your offer is tempting, but the risk is clear. I'll need some time to think it over carefully before parting with my coins.'

The lesson: whenever a borrower promises returns that feel too good to be true, the investor must examine the risks closely before investing.

Some Things to Consider While Making Your Choice

When picking a fixed-income investment, think about the CTRL (control) key on your keyboard:

- **C for Credit Risk:** Is the borrower reliable? Government-backed options are safer, but higher returns from corporate bonds or FDs come with more risk – always check the credit ratings of your borrower. A credit rating in a bond is an assessment of the issuer's ability to repay debt, indicating the risk of default. Agencies like CRISIL, ICRA and CARE assign ratings from AAA (highest safety) to D (default). Higher-rated bonds offer lower yields, while lower-rated bonds carry higher risk, but may provide better returns.
- **T for Tenure:** How long can you lock away your

investment? FDs and debt mutual funds offer shorter terms, while PPFs and bonds are long-term. Choose an investment that matches the timeline in which you need your money.
- **R for Return:** Higher returns often mean higher risk, especially in case of corporate bonds. Balance risk with your need for steady income.
- **L for Liquidity:** How fast can you cash out your investment without incurring penalties? FDs and debt funds offer more flexibility than PPF or bonds.

Always remain in CTRL – Credit, Tenure, Return, and Liquidity – to keep your investments in check!

When you're putting money into fixed-income investments, don't just look at the big, shiny pre-tax return number. The post-tax return is what really matters because taxes can eat into returns more than you might anticipate. Sometimes, a slightly lower pre-tax return on tax-efficient options like PPF, or National Savings Certificate, can actually leave you with more in your pocket, depending on your income tax bracket.

Types of Fixed-Income Instruments

Type of Instrument	To Whom You Are Lending	What You Get
Government Bonds	Government	Low-risk, steady interest payments backed by the government

Type of Instrument	To Whom You Are Lending	What You Get
Corporate Bonds	Corporations	Higher returns but with increased credit risk
Bank Fixed Deposits (FDs)	Banks	Guaranteed interest over a fixed tenure with safety and predictable returns
Small Savings Schemes	Government-backed schemes	Guaranteed returns, tax benefits like 80C, long-term security through schemes like PPF, NSC, SCSS
Company Fixed Deposits	Corporations	Higher interest rates than bank FDs, but with greater credit risk

If tracking credit ratings and picking investments feels like too much work, don't worry! You can let the pros handle it by investing in a **debt mutual fund** (more on this later). It's like hiring a personal curator for your money – they do the hard work and choose the best options for you, while you enjoy the returns stress-free.

Tip: A higher interest rate always comes with some level of risk. When in doubt, check the borrower's credit rating.

How to Make the Most of Your Fixed-Income Portfolio

Shreyasi, a forty-one-year-old schoolteacher, liked the security offered by FDs to cater to her short-term needs – paying the kids' school fees, their annual family trip to hill stations and an emergency fund. She'd gather up her savings and put them into one big FD for five years without much thought. But one day, while she was at the bank, she overheard a new term: FD laddering. Curious, she asked to meet her advisor, Anirban, for tea to learn more.

'*Arey* Shreyasi *di*, it's simple,' Anirban said. 'Instead of locking ₹5 lakh into one long-term FD, you just split it up – put ₹1 lakh in a one-year FD, another ₹1 lakh in a two-year one, and so on. That way, one matures every year and if interest rates go up, you can reinvest the matured amount into a new deposit and earn better interest.'

'So I'll get greater flexibility to withdraw or reinvest my money, regularly have access to my invested amount and even benefit from higher rates if they improve?'

'Exactly! Plus you can use this method with bonds or company deposits too,' Anirban said.

Learning about 'laddering' helped Shreyasi see a new way to improve her returns. Laddering has some clear advantages. First, it helps you weather the ups and downs of interest rates – if the rates go up, you can put your matured FD into a better-paying one, and if they go down, your longer-term FDs are still locked in at higher rates. Secondly, it gives you regular access to your money without having to break your long-term deposits prematurely.

Example of FD Laddering

FD Number	Investment Amount (₹)	Tenure	Interest Rate (%)
1st FD	1 lakh	1 year	6.50
2nd FD	1 lakh	2 years	6.75
3rd FD	1 lakh	3 years	7
4th FD	1 lakh	4 years	7.25
5th FD	1 lakh	5 years	7.50

Upon maturity, you can simply reinvest the amount at the new five-year rate.

Fixed-income products are an uncomplicated and predictable way of growing your money with low risk, despite the lower returns. True to its name, the role of fixed-income products is to generate fixed returns by lending to someone trustworthy – hence it is paramount to ensure that that someone is the right borrower. For higher returns and more excitement, there are always equities to invest in – and that's what's coming up next!

KEY LEARNINGS

- Fixed income won't make you rich overnight, but it won't break you either.
- If the promised returns sound too good to be true, they probably are. When in doubt, look closely at the credit risks of an investment.
- Long lock-ins without liquidity can be a financial headache. Ladder your FDs for better returns.

Resources

- As of 14 February 2025, the details for various savings schemes in India are as follows:

Scheme	Lock-in Period	Interest Rate (as of 1 January 2025) (in % per annum)	Maximum Investment Limit	Taxation	Key Features
Post Office Monthly Income Scheme (POMIS)	5 years	7.4	₹9 lakh (single account); ₹15 lakh (joint account)	Interest is taxable; TDS applicable as per prevailing laws	Provides a fixed monthly income. Minimum investment of ₹1,000. Premature withdrawal allowed after 1 year with a penalty.

Scheme	Lock-in Period	Interest Rate (as of 1 January 2025) (in % per annum)	Maximum Investment Limit	Taxation	Key Features
Kisan Vikas Patra (KVP)	Matures in 120 months (10 years)	7.5	No upper limit	Interest is taxable; TDS applicable as per prevailing laws	Investment doubles in 120 months. Available in denominations of ₹1,000, ₹5,000, ₹10,000, and ₹50,000. Premature encashment allowed after 2.5 years.
5-Year National Savings Certificate (NSC)	5 years	7.7	No upper limit	Eligible for tax deduction under Section 80C; interest is taxable	Minimum investment of ₹1,000. Provides guaranteed returns. Suitable for risk-averse investors.
Senior Citizen Savings Scheme (SCSS)	5 years (extendable by 3 years)	8.2	₹30 lakh	Interest is taxable; TDS applicable if interest exceeds ₹50,000 per annum	Exclusively for individuals aged 60 and above. Offers high safety and regular income. Premature closure allowed after 1 year with a penalty.

Scheme	Lock-in Period	Interest Rate (as of 1 January 2025) (in % per annum)	Maximum Investment Limit	Taxation	Key Features
Sukanya Samriddhi Yojana (SSY)	21 years from account opening or until the girl's marriage after the age of eighteen	8.2	₹1.5 lakh per financial year	Eligible for tax deduction under Section 80C; interest and maturity amount are tax-free	For girl children below 10 years. Minimum deposit of ₹250 per year. Partial withdrawal allowed after the girl turns 18.
Public Provident Fund (PPF)	15 years (extendable in blocks of 5 years)	7.1	₹1.5 lakh per financial year	Eligible for tax deduction under Section 80C; interest and maturity amount are tax-free	Long-term investment with compounding benefits. Minimum deposit of ₹500 per year. Partial withdrawals allowed from year 7.

Please note that interest rates are subject to periodic revisions by the Government of India. It is advisable to consult with a financial advisor or refer to official government publications for the most current information.

12

EQUITIES

Owning Tata without the Tension

Faced with the imminent collapse of the airline she worked for, air hostess Jasmine Kohli dreamed of ditching the daily grind to start her own beauty business. Sounds glamorous, right? But well, starting up isn't all lipsticks and luxury. In fact, it's a maze of paperwork, regulations and stress. In the 2024 movie, *Crew*, Jasmine (played by Kareena Kapoor) even considers hijacking a plane to fund her dreams – but thankfully, only in reel life!

Don't worry – you don't need to plan a daring money heist to realize your dreams of owning a flourishing business. Actually, what if I told you there was a way you could own a piece of the most well-established businesses without any of the hassle of running them? That is precisely what equities can offer you. In this chapter, you'll learn how equities can provide you with many of the biggest benefits of owning a business empire without any of the headaches. Let's dive into the basics.

What Are Equities?

If it is so hard to run one beauty business, imagine having to run a luxury and lifestyle company like Titan, or a pharmaceutical company like Lupin, or a bank like Federal Bank, or a global automobile manufacturer like Tata Motors – all at the same time! Sounds impossible, right? But what if you could gain part ownership of these firms and a slice of their profits?

Equities, often referred to as **stocks** or **shares**, represent ownership in a company. When you buy equity share of a company, you're essentially buying a small part of that company, becoming, in market jargon, a shareholder. This ownership entitles you to a portion of the company's profits (if and when they come in), through two methods: period paybacks, known as dividends, which companies are required to pay their shareholders, and two, price appreciation. The latter means that you benefit from owning higher-priced shares of a company showing consistent profit growth.

Titan, Lupin, Tata Motors – they all went on to become stocks that multiply in value several times, also known as **multi-baggers**. Legendary investor, Rakesh Jhunjhunwala, had purchased equities in all of them (amongst many other companies), and was rewarded with the immense wealth these stocks generated for their investors – and never had to worry about running any of them!

Benefits of Equity Investing

During the wedding season in Delhi, one of our relatives – let's call him Mr Finer Things – was boasting at a family lunch about having spent ₹3 crores on his son's reception. *₹3 crores on a wedding?!* I rolled my eyes. The menu, of course, was Delhi's staple: dal makhani and shahi paneer. Decades ago, each plate might have cost the hosts ₹1,000, but now, thanks to inflation, it had risen to nearly ₹6,000, plus taxes, plus, plus, plus …

Renu, a family friend who had overhead this conversation, suddenly turned to me and asked, 'This increase in per plate cost is crazy! How do we even beat such inflation?'

'Inflation is here to stay,' I said. 'We might as well invite it to the table to be a guest.'

The follow-up question came quickly: 'How?'

'Well, by investing in companies which benefit from inflation – like food producers. This could turn rising costs into rising profits. For example, a leading food company's stock rose from ₹330 in 2019 to ₹575 in 2024, a 73 per cent gain.'

Equities, I explained, historically gave 12 per cent average returns over long term, beating inflation and outpacing gold, real estate *and* fixed deposits. The government also fundamentally wants equities as an asset class to do well as its success is a reflection of the state of the economy and boosts their own tax revenue through capital gains tax. With the emerging online brokerage platforms, investing in equities has become as easy as gulping down a third serving of gulab jamuns at a wedding reception.

By the time our desserts arrived, Renu seemed less troubled by inflation, and Mr Big Spender looked like he was mulling over redirecting a portion of his massive catering budget into equities.

Risks of Equity Investing

Renu was visibly excited to jump into equities halfway through our conversation. But I was careful to keep her grounded. Equities, too, came with their own share of risks and it was time to broach that subject with her. Her eyebrows arched in response.

'Risks? What risks?'

'Let's start with volatility,' I said.

I know, I know. It sounds like a big word, but simply, it means that stock prices can swing wildly. Some days, business booms; on others, it doesn't, and sometimes, losses also pile up. During the COVID-19 pandemic, markets plunged by 30–40 per cent as businesses shuttered. Think of the hotel industry's struggles with empty dining rooms during that time! But markets also rebounded once things normalized. Even during major downturns like the pandemic, sectors like healthcare can thrive, highlighting how various industries respond differently to market shifts.

'Equities perform well in the long term,' I said,

summing it up, though not without another word of caution: 'But in the short run, you could lose money. If a company you invested in doesn't perform well – or worse, goes bankrupt – you could lose the capital you've invested.'

For instance, Air Deccan, India's first low-cost airline, revolutionized air travel in the early 2000s, but financial struggles led to the company ceasing operations in 2020, leaving its investors high and dry.

'Then there is market risk, when the entire market takes a hit,' I continued. 'You could own stocks in ten different companies but if the entire economy sees a slump, your portfolio too will feel it.'

While markets eventually recover in the long run, there are also sector-specific risks to account for. For example, if you were invested heavily in oil companies when the prices had plummeted in 2020, your investments would have taken a big hit.

'All this is a little scary,' Renu admitted.

'Yep. But there is a way around it: diversification. Spreading your investments across sectors is crucial,' I said. 'You don't want to put all your investments in one sector. If you were an emperor of different kingdoms, when one struggled, another might thrive in a different part of your empire. You wouldn't want to risk emptying your royal treasury because of the issues affecting one kingdom, would you?'

Renu nodded. 'I see your point. Alright, with that,' she declared, 'I think I'm ready to start my equity investment journey, and I'm gearing up for a bumpy ride.'

How Can You Start Investing in Equities?

After a long day at work, I was sitting in the car on my way home, staring into the sea of red taillights before me. The city felt like it was moving in slow motion, but my patience was already at full sprint toward the finish line. Out of the blue, my driver asked, 'Madam, I heard Tesla's coming to India. Should I invest in EV stocks?'

What?! I couldn't help but smile. Here we were, trudging miserably through peak-hour traffic, and he was thinking about stocks. Although equity investing is rising overall, most Indian households still invest only about 5 per cent of their savings into stocks, as compared to over 20 per cent in the US.

For those of you who want to start investing in equities, choose one of two paths: either go hands-on with your own demat account and pick your stocks, or opt for mutual funds. But let's be honest – everyone now thinks they're the Wolf of Dalal Street, setting up fancy monitors and chasing after stock tips. But stock-picking requires real knowledge and without that, those screens are but expensive decor items and your portfolio much less likely to yield any real profits.

Mutual funds, on the other hand, are like hiring a skilled driver. They spread your money across stocks and manage your portfolio professionally, so you can sit back and relax without getting into the nitty-gritty of it all – a smoother, safer ride, even for the wariest of investors.

Equity mutual funds and stocks are a great way of earning good returns on your investments, but like with all investments, it is important to manage your expectations. I remember a time when my father got a 60 per cent return on his investments in a single year. It was a fantastic time, but I was compelled to caution him, 'This won't happen every year'.

Like good friendships, equities require time and patience. Trying to get rich overnight only sets you on the course for disappointment. In October 2024, a conman scammed hundreds in Dibrugarh, Assam with promises of huge returns through a bogus trading scheme, leaving investors devastated. Even in legitimate trading, many dive into high-risk Futures and Options (F&O), hoping for quick gains, while forgetting that trading is risky and can lead to massive losses. Nine out of ten traders lose money, be warned.

Investing takes time, just like writing a bestseller. You have to build the story chapter by chapter and let the organic plot twist of compound interest create a spectacular finale over time.

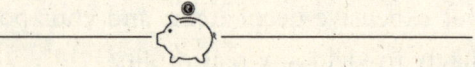

Tip: The stock market isn't a casino, and it punishes those who treat it as such.

Well-regulated and Organized Market

Films and web series like *Scam* (1992) often sensationalize the stock market, painting it as a playground for scams and manipulation. After all, cons do make for thrilling entertainment – who wouldn't want to watch a high-stakes drama? But this dramatic portrayal isn't just confined to movies and shows. On social media, I often come across posts screaming about how stocks are a scam or Initial Public Offerings (IPOs) are a scam. Such videos are often created to grab attention and incite fear or cause confusion.

But where are the blockbusters or viral videos about iconic brands and massive wealth creators like Infosys, DMart or Indigo? I guess no drama means no story. My advice to you is to not take everything at face value. Understand the regulations and investor protection mechanisms in place to keep the market fair and transparent. India's stock market might have its share of drama, but let me tell you, it's no Wild West.

SEBI keeps a sharp eye on things, ensuring transparency and protecting investors. Remember the Yes Bank crisis in 2020? SEBI stepped in, restricted short-selling to curb manipulation, and backed a rescue plan to help steady the ship. And in case of Kingfisher Airlines, it didn't hesitate to bar Vijay Mallya from the market and corporate boards for financial misconduct.

There is no denying that the market has its twists and turns, but behind the scenes, there is a solid system of checks and balances in place. So the next time someone tells you the stock market is just a big scam, remind them it's not the drama but the quiet, steady supervisory powers that keep India's equity market running in the first place.

How to Be a Better Equity Investor

Imagine borrowing money from your parents to start a business selling vintage sneakers online. You pour your heart into it – building an app, setting up drop-shipping, sourcing rare sneakers from every corner of the internet, an inventory all lined up, a snazzy interface, and a solid launch plan. Your minimum viable product is ready for launch – a process that will take *months*, not days!

Just as the first orders start trickling in, the big question from your parents comes crashing down onto your dreams: 'When will we get our money back?'

Thing is, there's no way around it. You'll have to convince your parents that building a business takes time; it's not a magic wand that conjures up profits overnight. There will be days when orders trickle in; weeks that feel like uphill climbs, and even entire seasons when nothing seems to be going the right way. Growth happens in the long term.

It's the same with equities: they don't hand out dividends on demand. But if you respect the process, equities will reward you. Or as Marilyn Monroe is famously quoted to say: 'If you can't handle me at my worst, you surely don't deserve me at my best.'

> **KEY LEARNINGS**
>
> - Equities create long-term wealth by beating inflation and providing superior returns as compared to other asset classes.
> - Market volatility is normal. Stocks rise and fall, but long-term investors come out ahead.
> - Diversification reduces risk. Spread investments across sectors to avoid heavy losses during downturns.

PART III

MAKING MONEY WORK FOR YOU

13

MUTUAL FUNDS I

Welcome to the Financial Food Court

Imagine a group of friends pooling their money to buy a variety of dishes at a food court. Each person gets to enjoy the entire spread without having to pay for every dish individually. Mutual funds work similarly by pooling investors' money to create a diversified portfolio. They are one of the simplest and most cost-effective ways to invest in various asset classes, including equities, debt, commodities and Real Estate Investment Trusts (REITs) or Infrastructure Investment Trust (INVITs). They are designed to cater to all kinds of investors with different financial goals, risk appetites and time horizons.

Let's explore what makes mutual funds a preferred investment choice – here's the menu!

What Are Mutual Funds?

Mutual funds pool money from multiple investors to invest in a diversified portfolio of assets and are managed by professional fund managers, who allow investors to benefit from expertise, diversification and economies of scale. Think of them as a shared taxi ride. Instead of each person paying their own full taxi fares and getting separate taxis (investing directly in individual securities), they contribute a part of the shared taxi's fare (mutual fund) and everyone reaches their destination efficiently.

Why Mutual Funds?

Investing directly in the stock market is like baking your own bread – you need to source ingredients, follow recipes and put in effort. Mutual funds are like buying bread from an expert baker – convenient, consistent and professionally crafted.

- **Cost-effective:** Economical compared to direct investing due to shared costs.
- **Well-regulated:** Governed by SEBI, ensuring investor protection.
- **Professionally managed:** Managed by experts with deep market insights.
- **Popular:** One of the most preferred investment vehicles globally.

What Makes Mutual Funds Safer?

Mutual funds are like a chauffeur-driven car that you can relax in the back of while the expert takes care of navigating traffic, ensuring a safe and smooth journey.

- **Tightly Regulated by SEBI:** Robust regulations and regular audits ensure transparency.
- **Trust Structure:** Assets are held by an independent trustee to safeguard investors.
- **Ownership of Units:** Investors own mutual fund units proportionate to their investment amount.

Types of Mutual Funds

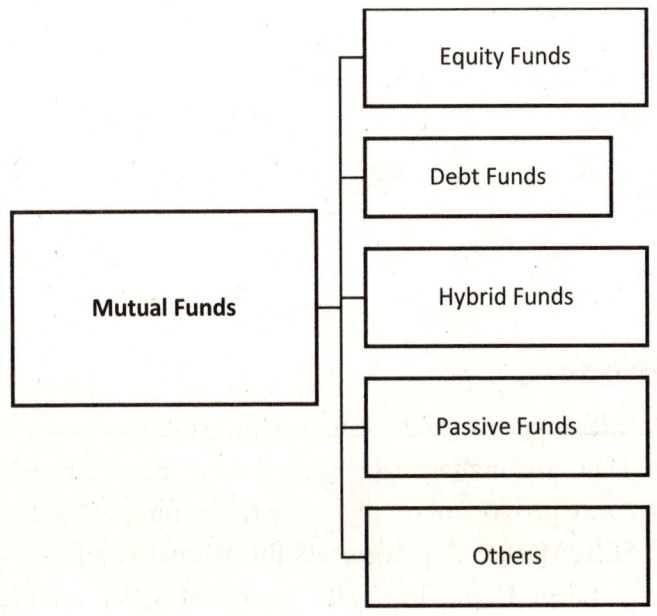

Equity Funds

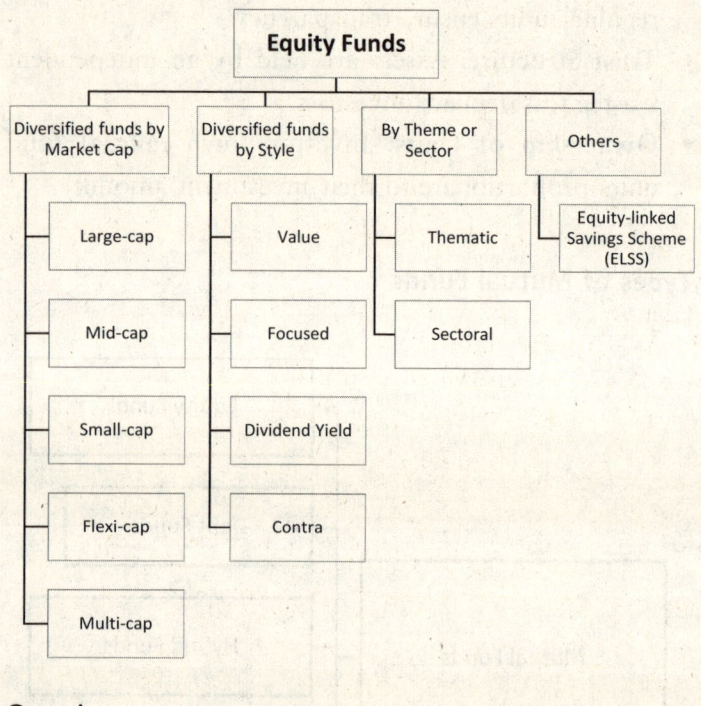

Overview

- These type of funds primarily invest in stocks.
- They are managed by skilled fund managers who construct portfolios aligned with the fund's objective.
- **SEBI Market Cap Segments for Mutual Funds**
  - **Large-Cap:** Top 100 companies by market capitalization.
    - Large, stable businesses, relatively moderate risk, steady growth.
  - **Mid-Cap:** Companies ranked between 101–250 by market capitalization.

- ■ Medium-scale businesses, growth potential, high risk.
- **Small-Cap:** Companies ranked 250 and below.
  - ■ Emerging businesses, high growth potential, very high risk.

Types

As per SEBI's Scheme Categorization rules, equity mutual funds are divided based on four broad criteria: market cap, style of investment, theme or sector of investment and other basis. This detailed categorization offers investors the flexibility to choose funds based on their market capitalization preferences, investment style and focus areas, while ensuring their ambitions for the funds align with their risk appetites and return objectives.

Think of equity funds like choosing teams in cricket – you need a balance of batters, bowlers and all-rounders to win a match. Equity funds work on the same principle: they balance large-cap (stable players), mid-cap (rising stars) and small-cap (aggressive performers) by varying ratios to help you hit your target score like a champ! Here's what you need to know about all the types:

Diversified Funds Categorized by Market Cap

Large-cap fund	Mid-cap fund	Small-cap fund	Flexi-cap fund	Multi-cap fund
Minimum 80% investment in large-cap stocks (Top 100 companies)	Minimum 65% investment in mid-cap stocks (Rank 101–250 companies)	Minimum 65% investment in small-cap stocks (Rank 251 onwards).	Minimum 65% investment in equity across all market caps without restrictions	Minimum 25% each in largecap, mid-cap and small-cap stocks

Diversified Funds Categorized by Style

Value fund	Focused fund	Dividend Yield fund	Contra fund
Minimum 65% investment in equity following a value investing strategy	• Invest in a maximum of 30 stocks across market caps with no sectoral limits • Minimum 65% in equity	Minimum 65% investment in dividend-yielding stocks.	Minimum 65% in equity using a contrarian investment strategy (buying undervalued sectors/stocks)

Funds Categorized by Sector or Theme

Sectoral fund	Thematic fund
• Minimum 80% investment in a specific sector • Examples: – Technology Funds – Banking & Financial Services Funds – Healthcare & Pharma Funds – Infrastructure Funds – Real Estate Funds	• Minimum 80% investment in stocks aligned to a specific theme • Examples: – ESG Funds – Rural Development Funds – Consumption Funds – Global Opportunities Funds

Other Categories of Equity Funds

Equity-linked Savings Scheme (ELSS)
• Minimum 80% in equity with a three-year lock-in period • Provides tax benefits under Section 80C

The Investment Checklist

☐ Evaluate the fund management team.
☐ Assess the fund's long-term performance and processes.
☐ Ensure a blend of different styles/types for diversification.

Fixed-income Funds

Fixed-income funds primarily invest in fixed-income securities such as bonds, treasury bills, commercial papers and money market instruments. They are ideal for conservative investors seeking stability, regular income and lower risk compared to equities.

Types

Type	Features	Suitable for	Risk Profile
Liquid and Ultra-short Duration funds	• Invest in very short-term debt instruments with maturities up to 91 days (Liquid Funds) or a portfolio duration of 3–6 months (Ultra-short Funds). • Generally higher returns than savings accounts	Suitable for parking idle cash or managing short-term liquidity	Minimal risk with high liquidity
Short-Term funds (e.g. Short Duration Funds, Low Duration Funds)	Invest in debt instruments with a maturity period of 0–3 years	Ideal for investors with a short investment horizon who seek better returns than fixed deposits	Moderate, with some exposure to interest rate and credit risks

Type	Features	Suitable for	Risk Profile
Long-term funds (e.g. Gilt Funds, Dynamic Bond Funds)	Invest in debt instruments with longer maturities, usually over 5 years	Designed for investors seeking higher returns over an extended period	Higher sensitivity to interest rate changes, making them riskier than short-term funds
Target Maturity funds (e.g. Bharat Bond ETFs, PSU SLD TMF)	Passive fixed-income funds that invest in bonds with a fixed maturity date, often aligned with its benchmark	Offer predictable returns for investors looking for a long-term, FD-like alternative	Lower risk if held till maturity, as they eliminate interest rate volatility

What to Expect

- **Stability and regular income**
  - Fixed-income funds provide a relatively stable investment option with regular interest payouts.
  - Suitable for risk-averse investors or as a diversification tool in a portfolio.
- **Lower risk compared to equities**
  - Fixed-income funds carry less volatility and are less affected by market fluctuations compared to equity funds.

Risks

- **Credit risk (default risk)**
  - Risk of the bond issuer defaulting on interest

payments or principal repayment.
- Lower-rated securities may offer higher yields but carry a greater risk of default.
- **Interest rate risk**
  - The risk of bond prices falling when interest rates rise.
  - Longer-duration funds are more sensitive to interest rate changes, while short-duration funds are less affected.
- **Liquidity risk**
  - The risk of not being able to redeem investments quickly due to low trading activity in certain securities.
- **Reinvestment risk**
  - Risk of having to reinvest proceeds at lower interest rates when bonds mature during declining rate cycles.

Fixed-income funds cater to investors with varying risk appetites and investment horizons. They provide a flexible alternative to fixed deposits while offering potential for better returns and liquidity. However, **investors should carefully assess the risks – particularly credit and interest rate risks –** to align with their financial goals.

Hybrid Funds

Hybrid funds provide a comprehensive investment solution by blending asset classes to suit different risk profiles and financial objectives. Whether you're a conservative investor or an aggressive one, there's a hybrid fund tailored to your needs.

Hybrid funds combine investments across asset classes like equity, debt and sometimes alternative assets (gold, REITs, etc.). These funds aim to balance risk and reward, offering growth potential with stability. They are ideal for investors seeking diversification in a single product.

Types

Type	Features	Risk Profile	Suitable for
Arbitrage Funds	• These funds exploit price differences between cash (stocks) and derivatives (futures) markets to generate returns. • Minimum 65% in equity and equity-related instruments, with the remainder in debt/money market instruments. • Comparable to short-term fixed-income funds but taxed like equity funds.	Low risk due to hedging strategies.	Low-risk investors looking for for tax-efficient short-term parking.

Equity + Debt Hybrid Funds

Type	Features	Risk Profile	Suitable for
Balanced Advantage Funds (Dynamic Asset Allocation Funds)	• Dynamically manage exposure to equity and fixed income based on market conditions. • No fixed allocation; can vary equity–debt proportion from 0% to 100%.	Moderate risk, changes with investment mix.	Investors seeking flexibility, aiming for equity-like returns with lower volatility and market-driven returns.
Aggressive Hybrid Funds	• Primarily equity-oriented, investing 65–80% in equity and the remainder in debt. • Ideal for investors with a higher risk appetite and longer investment horizon.	High risk because of more equity exposure.	Investors looking for higher returns than traditional bonds or FDs and can also handle moderate volatility in returns.
Equity Savings Funds	• Invest in a mix of equity, debt and arbitrage opportunities. • Minimum 65% in equity (including arbitrage) and the rest in debt.	Moderate risk	Conservative investors looking for regular income with equity tax benefits.
Multi-Asset Funds	• Diversified funds investing in at least three different asset classes (eg., equity, debt and gold or silver).	Moderate to high risk, depending on asset mix	Investors who want diversification to balance between risk and returns

Type	Features	Risk Profile	Suitable for
	• Minimum 10% in each asset class. • Reduces risk through broad diversification while tapping into multiple growth opportunities.		

Key Benefits

- **Diversification:** Since your investments are distributed across multiple asset classes, the impact of poor performance in a single asset class is minimized.
- **Risk-adjusted Returns:** Balances the high growth potential of equity with the stability of debt.
- **Tax Efficiency:** Funds with 65 per cent or more equity allocation enjoy equity taxation benefits, making them more tax-efficient than pure debt funds.
- **Investing Simplified:** A single product that caters to varied financial goals, reducing the need for multiple investments.

Passive Funds

McDonald's is for when you're not in the mood to think too much about what you would like to satisfy your hunger with. Whether you are in Mumbai or Manali, those burgers and fries will taste the same. Passive funds work the same way – they comprise index funds and exchange traded funds (ETFs), which offer low-cost investing without the hassle of stock-picking.

Index funds are like a standard meal combo. They track a market index like Nifty 50, giving steady, no-fuss returns. ETFs do the same, but trade like stocks, with prices changing throughout the day, based on demand.

Key Benefits

- They cost lower than actively managed funds.
- Returns closely match the underlying index, so they are easier to track.

Other Funds

There are yet other types of mutual funds for investors looking for wider diversification.

International Funds

These allow for exposure to global markets. It's like taking a trip abroad – you are exposed to different cultures (markets) and broaden your horizons.

Fund of Funds

These invest in other mutual funds for added diversification and is like hiring a travel planner to arrange your entire trip – you'll get to enjoy the experience without worrying about the nitty-gritty or logistics.

Mutual funds are versatile tools that aim to cater to every type of investor. Whether you seek high growth, steady income, or a mix of both – there's a mutual fund option tailored for you. Understanding your options and the differences between the various types can really help you make informed investment decisions. Think of it like planting a garden. You can grow flowers for the beauty (equities), vegetables for sustenance (debt), and trees for long-term stability (hybrid) – and they will all be cared for expertly by an experienced gardener.

14

MUTUAL FUNDS II

Maruti or Mercedes – What's Your Ride?

Determined to stay true to his New Year's resolution, Varun finally stepped into a gym. Imported treadmills gleamed under the bright lights. Posters of Arnold Schwarzenegger and Ronnie Coleman flexing their rippling muscles adorned the walls. Inspired, Varun strolled up to the trainer. '*Bhaiyya*, what's the best exercise?' he asked.

The trainer smiled. 'Best for what?'

'Umm … everything?'

'There's no best exercise. You want to lose weight? Do cardio. Build muscle? Do strength training. Improve flexibility? Do Yoga. And if you want overall fitness, mix it all up.'

The trainer was right.

Similarly, people ask me, 'Which is the best mutual fund?'

Just like there is no best exercise, **there is no best**

mutual fund. Some funds are like cardio, steady and reliable (debt funds). Others are like weight training; high risks and high rewards (equity funds). And then there are balanced funds, offering a mix of both. The best mutual fund for you depends on what your goals, risk appetite and time horizon are.

Just like fitness plans differ by body type, investments must match your financial personality type. In this chapter, we'll guide you through the key factors to consider when choosing the right mutual fund.

Why Picking a Fund Is Like Buying a Car

Imagine walking into a car showroom and realising that buying a car is not one single factor purchase decision. Komal Mehta's boutique business was growing, and she was done cramming fabric rolls into her tiny hatchback. It was time for an SUV. But at the showroom, she quickly realized picking a car meant evaluating factors like maintenance, safety, mileage, resale value and a lot more.

Mutual funds work the same way. People tend to choose the one offering the highest returns in recent years. Once you've decided to invest in mutual funds, be it equity or debt, the real question you need to ask yourself is: which one actually fits your requirements? Here are a few things you should consider before investing in mutual funds:
- Rolling returns

- Fund manager consistency
- Exit load
- Expense ratio

Let's see what we can learn from Komal's experience of buying the right car for herself.

'How Much Maintenance Does It Need?'

One SUV looked perfect, but when Komal asked about its long-term reliability, the salesman hesitated. It performed great in the first few years, but engine issues had been reported in past models and the repairs could add up over time.

In the context of mutual funds, this shiny SUV compares to point-to-point returns, which show how much an investment grew between two fixed dates, like 1 January to 31 December in a given year. Sounds simple enough, but this can be very misleading if it is the only factor you look at. If the market went through a lucky phase just before the end date, a fund might boast a flashy 25 per cent return even after having struggled all year.

This is why **rolling returns** are a better criterion to judge performance over time. They smooth out short-term fluctuations by averaging returns over multiple overlapping periods. For example, a fund with 12 per cent rolling returns over five years means that it has consistently hovered around that return, no matter which five-year period you take into account. Another fund with the same five-year return but wild swings between 30 per cent one year and 2 per cent another meant higher unpredictability and lower average returns.

Most websites will display point-to-point returns by default. Make sure you do your homework and check rolling returns to get a better picture of a fund's performance before you buy and set your return expectations.

'What Are the Safety Features?'

Komal liked the look of another SUV at the showroom. She enquired about its safety features and the salesman's enthusiasm snuffed out. The company had recalled it three times in five years, he told her. It looked great, but there was no reliable guarantee that passengers would be safe if it got into an accident.

In case of mutual funds, the safety feature you need to check for is your fund manager. A fund's performance depends on who's managing it. If the fund manager keeps changing, the strategy and returns it offers will also vary as different managers will have different styles, risk appetites and stock-picking approaches. Frequent change in managers can lead to instability – it is ideal if a fund manager has been looking after a fund for at least three years.

'What About Its Resale Value?'

Komal had almost settled on a model when she remembered she hadn't checked on its resale value. The salesman, excited at almost having sealed the deal, once again deflated. It would lose half its worth in four years, he told her. No way was Komal going to buy a car that was expensive to buy but tough to re-sell.

Similarly in case of mutual funds, you are charged a fee for pulling out money before a certain date as a subtle deterrent. If you don't want to pay this fee, you would have to invest for a longer term. Equity funds often charge a 1 per cent exit load if redeemed (withdrawn) within a year. This may not sound like a big deal, but it needs to be something you are aware about at the time of purchase. Debt funds usually have lower or no exit loads at all, making them more flexible. Some funds follow a graded system – 1 per cent for the first six months, 0.5 per cent for the next six, and zero after a year.

'How's the Mileage?'

Komal was just beginning to give up hope when another flashy SUV caught her eye. She asked the salesman about its mileage and the salesman told her it was not the best in that sphere. The more she drove, the more it would cost her since it consumed a lot of fuel.

The mutual fund equivalent is the expense ratio, or

the fee you are charged for the management of your investment. Equity funds have higher expense ratios (1–2.25 per cent) since they require active management, while debt funds have lower ones (0.5–1 per cent) since their returns are lower and they cannot charge higher fees.

Automatic or Manual?

For years, automatic cars were a luxury. No clutch, no gear shifts required. Today, they're everywhere, making life easier for people who love to cruise along in city traffic. Yet, some people still swear by manual cars. They love being in complete control and determining the precision with which their car moves.

Investing is no different. Passive funds are like automatic cars – they allow you to sit back and let the market do the work. They automatically adjust to match their returns against an index and once you invest, there's not much else for you to do. The advantages are clear:

- ✓ No fund managers needed to make decisions, so expense ratios remain low.
- ✓ The fund returns simply mirror indexes like Nifty 50 or Sensex.
- ✓ Follow the trends of the market, so there are no surprises.
- ✓ No need for frequent review.

> **REMEMBER**
>
> Imagine you're heading from home to work using GPS. The app says it will take you thirty minutes, but your actual time depends on traffic, detours and how well your driver is able to follow the route. If your driver makes many mistakes – like taking wrong turns, slowing down unnecessarily, or missing exits – they have a high **tracking error**.
>
> The time difference between the estimated and your real arrival time is known as the **tracking difference**. If GPS predicted thirty minutes, but you reach in thirty-five, that's a negative tracking difference, meaning you underperformed. If you get there in twenty-eight minutes, you have a positive tracking difference, meaning that you outperformed.
>
> For index funds and ETFs, the goal is to stick as close to the benchmark as possible, just like a good driver following the shortest, most efficient route. This means **you should strive for a low tracking error and low tracking difference**. Always look at tracking error and tracking difference of your passive fund before investing.

Active funds, on the other hand, are like manual cars. While you have fund managers to pick stocks with an

aim to beat the market, it takes effort and constant adjustment.
- ✓ Potential for higher returns. A skilled manager can outperform the market.
- ✓ Your portfolio will shift with market trends and opportunities.

But there are some caveats:
- Fund managers and analysts are top-notch, so expense ratios are higher.
- If the fund underperforms for too long, you have to decide whether you should switch.

So what's the best strategy? A mix of both! Just like some drivers switch between manual for control and automatic for ease, the smartest investment strategy blends active and passive funds.
- Use active funds where fund managers have a strong track record of beating the market.
- Use passive funds for low-cost, stress-free exposure to the overall market.

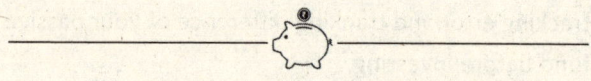

> **Tip:** Switching fund managers too often is like having a new captain on your team every season – things can get messy. Look for stability before investing.

Should You DIY or Consult an Expert?

Let's return to Komal for a moment, who'd finally found the right car and was now trying to hire a driver. Driving through Mumbai was pure chaos. Rickshaws cut into your lane like they owned the road and bikers squeezed through non-existent gaps, all while traffic jams turned a ten-minute drive into an hour-long test of patience. Even if you reached where you wanted on time, you would be more likely to stumble upon a mythical lost treasure than a parking spot.

Instead, she preferred to just sit back and scroll on her phone while someone else dealt with the madness. Having a driver would allow her to use those hours spent in traffic jams to be productive – working on new designs or catching up with her clients – but it would also mean giving up control. Driving herself would save money, but it also meant she'd have to deal with every pothole, every honk and every unexpected roadblock by herself.

Investing also works in a similar way.

A **regular plan** is like hiring a driver. It costs more, but you get expert guidance and someone else (your advisor) handles the twists and turns of the market. A **direct plan** is like driving yourself. Cost-effective, but you're in charge of everything. You pick the funds, track performance and make any necessary adjustments.

Both these approaches work – it is just a matter of preference whether you want to be in the driver's seat or enjoy the ride in the backseat. If you decide to go with a driver, we'll talk in greater detail about how to pick a good one in later chapters.

The User Manual

As Komal drove her new SUV home from the showroom, she reached into the glovebox and pulled out the car's user manual. It contained information about everything: mileage, service intervals, safety features, and even how to reset the music system if it froze. Makes sense, she thought. When you buy something as important as a car, you need to know how it works.

Mutual funds are no different. Each fund comes with a document outlining key details such as risks, historical returns, costs and other important details. The following information will help you decipher your **mutual fund manual**. These essential details can be found on the website of the AMC you buy from.

- **Risk-o-meter:** This tells you whether a fund is low, moderate, high or very high risk.
- **Net Asset Value (NAV):** This is the price per unit of a mutual fund. It's what you need to look out for to know what to pay when you are investing and what to expect you will get when you sell. Since it moves up and down with the market, it is a good indicator to gauge how your investment is faring.
- **Factsheet:** A factsheet is a snapshot of the fund's performance, top portfolio holdings like stocks or

bonds and expense ratio, and is typically published monthly.
- **Rulebook:** The Scheme Information Document (SID) includes detailed information about the fund's investment objective, investment strategy, asset allocation, risk factors, expense ratio and fund manager details.
- **Portfolio:** This offers a breakdown of where all your money is invested – from stocks and bonds to the various different sectors. AMCs also regularly share key changes in their portfolio strategy with investors via presentations and notes on their website.
- **Benchmark:** A benchmark is the yardstick used to measure a mutual fund's performance. This is usually set against a market index like Nifty 50 or Sensex for large-cap funds, or Nifty Midcap 150 for mid-cap funds. If your fund is consistently exceeding the benchmark, it's doing well. If it consistently lags behind, you might be better off investing in a passive fund that simply tracks the index and involves lower costs.
- **Growth or Payout:** Mutual funds offer two ways to handle your returns:
  - *Growth option:* Profits stay invested and compound over time, helping your money grow. Ideal for long-term wealth creation as there are no interim payouts.
  - *Income Distribution cum Capital Withdrawal (IDCW) option*: Returns are paid out at intervals,

similar to dividends in stocks. Suitable for those looking for passive income, but the payouts are not fixed and are taxable.

Mutual Fund Myth Busters

Somewhere between dinner-table advice, WhatsApp forwards and self-proclaimed market expert influencers, myths about mutual funds have taken on a life of their own. Some even sound logical, while others are either wishful thinking or simply inaccurate. Before you actually fall for them, let us bust some of these myths.

₹10 NAV > ₹100 NAV

Whether you cut your pizza into four big slices or eight smaller ones before you eat it, you will still end up eating the same amount of pizza. This is how NAV works in mutual funds. Buying a fund ₹10 NAV in a new fund offer (NFO) does not make it a better investment than another existing fund with a higher NAV. The per unit price is based on the fund's total assets, which means that a fund with ₹10 NAV and another with ₹100 NAV can deliver the same returns. Hence, instead of fixating on the NAV, focus on the other factors that can affect the growth of your money like fund performance, risk and expense ratio.

More Is Better

While spices in the right proportion can make a dish a lot better, dumping in everything in your kitchen drawer will certainly ruin it. Mutual funds work the same way. Having thirty funds in your portfolio does not mean better diversification. If you are invested in similar stocks, you are just adding complexity to your portfolio instead of reducing it. Most people do well with a few funds from each of the core asset classes and categories, and a portfolio of about ten mutual funds in total.

The Perfect Timing Exists

'*Market ka kya lagta hai*? (What do you think will happen with the market?)' People want to know whether the market will go up or down before they even invest. They believe that waiting for the *perfect* moment, if they time it just right, they can avoid all risk. But the truth is **the market will always go up and down.** There will never come a moment where everything is stable, predictable and risk-free. Invest when it is a good time for *you*.

The SIP Magic Wand

Ask ten people if they invest in mutual funds and you'll likely hear some of them say, 'No, I invest in SIPs'. Reality check: SIP, also known as a Systematic

Investment Plan, is not a separate investment. It is merely a method by which you can automate your investments by deducting a fixed amount from your bank account at regular intervals and putting it into a mutual fund of your choice. The fund you invest in – and not the SIP itself – determines your returns.

The Risk-free Index Fund

'I don't want to take any risk, so I'm investing in an index fund.' Sound familiar? *Sigh*. A lot of people assume index funds are some kind of safe haven – like a fixed deposit, but with better returns. Well, they're not. If you invest in a small-cap index fund and your friend picks a small-cap active fund, you're both essentially riding the same rollercoaster. If small caps crash, you will both take a hit. The only difference is that your friend's active fund might lose a little more or a little less money, depending on how well it is being managed.

Gym Trainer vs. YouTube Fitness Influencer

Remember Varun, who finally went to the gym? He once noticed a guy struggling under a squat rack – his form was off, and every few minutes, he paused to watch a YouTube tutorial. He was clearly winging his workout – much like DIY stock investors picking stocks without a clear strategy or technical know-how.

On the other hand, there were those who trained with

a trainer – they followed a structured plan and made steady progress, while avoiding injuries. This is how mutual fund investors fare when they let professionals handle the research, risk and execution part.

Just like training alone at the gym, direct stock investing requires:
- Daily research to track stocks, sectors and market trends
- Knowledge of financials, valuations and economic factors
- Discipline to stay invested even when stocks drop significantly
- Risk management through proper diversification and stop-loss strategies

If these words sound too big and like too much work for you, then skip the stock-picking and leave the heavy lifting to mutual funds!

The Gym Bro Who Overtrains

Varun spotted yet another character: an overconfident guy lifting more weight than he could handle. He grunted through a few shaky reps before dropping the bar noisily. He was like the traders who go after F&O chasing quick gains, but often getting hurt. F&O are tools that let you trade in the stock market by investing a smaller amount of money to control a bigger value of stocks. Think of it like paying a small deposit to book a car today, with the option to buy or sell it later at a set price.

Retail investors often use F&O to **speculate**, meaning they try to guess whether a stock or index will go up or down. If they guess right, the gains can be big because they're trading with more value than they actually paid for. But if they're wrong, the losses can also be big – sometimes more than the money invested. So while F&O can be exciting, they come with high risk and need careful understanding before jumping in.

A few things to note here:
- SEBI studies show that most traders lose money in F&O
- Short-term wins can be exciting, but long-term losses tend to pile up
- Sustainable progress beats risky shortcuts every time
- Leverage in F&O trading means that you are willing to take a much larger position than the money you actually have. This makes you prone to losing more than your capital, putting you in debt.

The gym had taught Varun one thing: a well-planned approach guarantees a win. Whether in fitness or investing, consistent growth is the real key to success.

Bad Bosses and Exit Strategies

Investing in a mutual fund can be a bit like starting a new job. Everything looks promising at first, but over time, things might change. Maybe the company isn't what it used to be, or maybe you outgrow it. Or maybe at the centre of all your issues is a bad boss – the mutual fund that no longer deserves your time.

So when should you quit a mutual fund?

The Excuse Machine

Your boss promised growth, exciting projects *and* a raise. Now, years later, all you keep getting is 'Let's revisit this in the next year'. Meanwhile, your friends have all got promotions or moved on to better jobs with 50 per cent hikes. Well, it's time to leave.

Similarly, a bad quarter or two is fine, but if a mutual fund lags behind its benchmark and peers consistently for three to five years, it's a dead-end fund. Compare long-term returns and if you find that your mutual fund keeps falling behind, it's time to walk away before it drags your portfolio down with it.

When You Outgrow It

You once loved the all-nighters for a critical presentation you absolutely nailed, but now, you are older and want work–life balance above all. But your boss still expects you to remain available till midnight. That's just not going to work.

Similarly, your financial goals too might change with time. Where you might once have preferred high-risk equity funds, you might now be looking for stability or a regular income, and your existing funds may no longer cut it. It's okay to move on.

The Rule Changer

You joined a stable company with clear goals. Then one day, new management arrived and suddenly, every team meeting is about 'reinventing the vision of the organization'. That can get tiring and is not the ideal situation for stability.

Similarly, funds might change. A stable large-cap investment may suddenly start taking more risks with mid-cap investments, or a new fund manager might completely alter the existing strategy. If your fund is suddenly playing a completely different game and you are not entirely comfortable with the new approach, it is time to revisit your portfolio.

Exit with a Plan, Not After an Emotional Outburst

Storming into your boss's office and quitting on the spot might feel great in your head, but it is a lot smarter an idea to plan your exit and go about it methodically in a balanced state of mind. The same goes for mutual funds. Review them regularly and walk away when they no longer serve you, but make sure your decision has a sound, objective basis. The right investment, like the right job, should help you grow – and never make you dread the hours you work!

> **KEY LEARNINGS**
>
> - Like workouts or cars, pick what fits your goals, risk and needs.
> - Cost, consistency and control matter.
> - Expense ratios, rolling returns and fund manager stability determine long-term success of mutual funds.
> - Invest smart, exit smarter. Drop bad funds like bad bosses before they deal any serious damage to your portfolio!

15

PORTFOLIO BUILDING

Lessons from The Great Indian Thali

On a sunny Sunday afternoon, my family and I decided to visit a restaurant known for its legendary thali. As the silver plate was on its way to our table, the tempting aroma had us swooning. The focus of the thali was the dal-chawal. Sabzis were lined neatly along the sides, behind three dots of chutney. There was a small portion of pickle. The rotis were perfectly warm. A bite-sized golden-brown gulab jamun awaited its turn towards the end of the meal.

No matter where I travel to, thalis always remind me of home. Dal, chawal, sabzi – their familiar aromas never fail to deliver a sense of comfort. It is no surprise that thalis are as popular as they are – cost-effective, adaptable to the needs of distinct regions and great nutritional value.

The philosophy of investing is not very different from that behind The Great Indian Thali. Building your financial thali – your portfolio – requires the mastery of the same balancing act that makes a thali great. Creating the right mix of stocks, bonds, gold and other instruments enables you to grow your wealth steadily without putting you under the stress of taking excessive risk. The act of creating this balance between risk and return in your portfolio is also known as asset allocation. Don't scratch your head just yet, we're only getting started!

What Is Asset Allocation?

Very simply, asset allocation is the process by which you decide what percentage of your funds you will allocate to which asset class – stocks, bonds, gold etc. – in your portfolio. Once they hear the word, the immediate question people often ask me is, 'What's the best asset allocation?'

The answer is: there isn't one. This is akin to asking what the best meal is. It is purely subjective. Your ideal meal, like your ideal asset allocation, depends on you – your goals, risk appetite and circumstances. You might prefer fiery Andhra spice to soothing Himachali flavours, or sadhya on a banana leaf in Kerala. Milk products commonly feature in our cuisine, but if you're lactose intolerant, you would want to skip the dairy. Similarly, your financial 'diet' should also cater to your preferences and sensitivities. The best thali – like the best portfolio – is the one tailored to meet your needs.

A good financial adviser can help you arrive at the right asset allocation for you so that even if one investment stumbles, others help you tide over the times with ease.

Types of Asset Allocation

Think of asset allocation like your diet. Dal chawal is an all-weather staple across India; a low-key hero that never lets you down. As a child, whenever I fell sick, my mother would cook up a comforting plate of dal chawal to ensure I stayed nourished and recovered sooner. It has remained at the core of my diet to this day. Similarly, your financial diet will also have a **core portfolio**. This is the dal chawal of your investments: something that has stood the test of time. Your core portfolio should ideally be built of long-term diversified funds like multi-cap funds, or large-cap and mid-cap index funds, or broad-based index funds. These are generally simple, timeless ideas that fit for all seasons.

Then comes your **satellite portfolio** – the chutney and dessert that add excitement and zest to the meal. During the course of your life, you might occasionally embark on exciting adventures like going for a scuba dive or attempting a triathlon. The satellite is like this little adventure: a smaller, dynamic portion of your investments to complement the stability of your core. These comprise the bold, opportunistic assets – sector-specific mutual funds and international stocks – that have the potential to offer higher returns but also come with greater volatility. And while a chutney can pack a punch, it is meant to be consumed in moderation and cannot comprise the bulk of your meal. The aggregate of these investments should ideally make up less than 20 per cent of your portfolio.

One of the most common mistakes people make while investing is to focus too much on their satellite portfolio. Many investors get distracted by the trees of which sector fund to buy or which fund in China to invest in, and sadly, lose sight of the woods. It's a bit like going on vacation, visiting a novel restaurant, only to end up having a two-hour conversation about the kind of oil they use and never even savouring your meal! Fact remains that the oil at that one restaurant won't affect your long-term health. But the oil you use at home? It matters a lot more because you consume it daily. The home oil is your core portfolio, which deserves the bulk of your time and attention. Once you get your core right, you won't need to worry about the rest – but even the spiciest chutney can't save a bad meal.

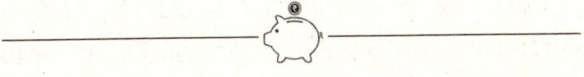

Tip: A good portfolio is like a great thali. Don't overdo the spice, and don't forget the staples.

How to Start Creating Your Portfolio

My nephew had just received a hefty bonus from his job in software engineering and was brimming with ideas. He told me about his three big dreams: a vacation to Europe in six months, saving for a house in three years, and building a retirement fund over twenty-five years.

'But where do I start?' he asked.

I introduced him to the **bucket approach**, which begins with breaking your goals down into smaller parts with clear timelines. For his vacation, I suggested he maintain liquid funds for safety and easy access. We allocated 10 per cent of his corpus to this. **For a short-term goal, it is best to not expose your wealth to market risk.**

For his house goal, we allocated 30 per cent to balanced advantage funds or BAFs. These are a type of mutual fund that dynamically adjust investments between equity (stocks) and debt (bonds) based on market conditions. They are designed to provide a balance of growth and stability, making them a popular choice for investors with moderate risk appetite. As for his retirement plans, we allocated 60 per cent for multi-cap and small-cap funds, which provide high returns but come with higher risk. Staying invested for a long term reduces the risk as markets generally recover from any dips in time, so it would ensure he is comfortable by the time his retirement comes around.

If you do not have a specific goal in mind for your

investment, your investment would typically fall in the long-term category. But if, for example, your goals would do well with an 80 per cent allocation to equities, but your risk appetite or psychology doesn't allow it, then you may want to temper your equity allocation down to a lower percentage. Remember: risk appetite differs from person to person. My father is a senior citizen, but he has a higher risk appetite with exposure to the market through equities, owing to his steady pension and fewer expenses. But I also know of colleagues at work in their mid-twenties, who are averse to market risk due to financial and family constraints. So asset allocation is highly personal and differs for each individual.

Rebalancing Your Portfolio

Amarjit Singh was the owner of a sports goods factory in Ludhiana. He was making good profits selling hockey sticks to retail outlets across India. Using his booming profits, he invested a good amount of money in the market in the post-COVID era, once the markets had recovered and were on a rise. Unsurprisingly, he had enjoyed what seemed like an endless bull run from 2022 to mid-2024.

In October 2024, however, the Indian stock market turned highly volatile due to weak corporate earnings, foreign investor removing money from Indian markets and a weakening rupee. Amarjit was desolate; he sat staring at the state of his investments. Equities in his portfolio had surged from 60 per cent to 80 per cent during the boom, but now they were dragging the overall value of his portfolio down. He had delayed what is known as 'rebalancing', thinking 'Why fix what isn't broken?'

But suddenly, everything had changed – this was a wake-up call. Amarjit realized that enjoying high returns without adjusting his portfolio was like skipping annual health check-ups. At first, everything feels fine, but over time, imbalances can creep in. And by the time you notice, damage may already have been done.

Just like regular health check-ups can catch issues early and keep you in good shape, rebalancing can help catch portfolio imbalances early on and keep your finances fit. Market fluctuations, like lifestyle changes, can throw things out of balance suddenly. Rebalancing is a reliable way of diagnosing and fixing any issues before they become problems, ensuring your financial goals stay on track.

When Should You Rebalance?

- **Scheduled Rebalancing:** You can schedule a reminder for reviewing and adjusting your portfolio once or twice a year. This will help keep things on track without letting emotions take over during the market ups and downs. Just don't overdo it – too much rebalancing can stack up transaction costs and taxes.
- **Deviation-based Rebalancing:** You can also watch for

major shifts in your portfolio, like a 5–10 per cent change from your target allocation, to revisit your allocations. For instance, if equities were supposed to comprise 60 per cent but now make up 70 per cent of your portfolio, thanks to market growth, it might be a good time to hit reset and get back to your original plan.
- **Life Events:** Big milestones like getting married, buying a house, having kids, or planning retirement can shake up your financial priorities. For this reason, they offer the perfect opportunities to pause and realign your portfolio to fit your new goals.

How Can You Rebalance?

- **How Much?** Start by reviewing your portfolio's total value. Figure out how much you need to tweak to get things back in line with your target allocations. For instance, Amarjit's portfolio was off by 20 per cent.
- **Where?** Compare your current allocation with your goals. For instance, if your portfolio went from 60 per cent equities and 40 per cent debt to 70 per cent equities and 30 per cent debt, rebalance by trimming equities and boosting debt to realign with your original targets.
- **What?** Keep a close watch on how your funds are doing. If some are underperforming, it might be time to swap them out for stronger options that will still match your goals and risk level. But stay invested in

a fund for at least three years before you compare its returns to its peers in the same category and judge its performance. If the fund is beating the benchmark and the average of funds in its category, you can continue to hold on.

Guidelines for Choosing Investment Products

As mentioned before, your financial goals should match your risk appetite and time horizon. Risk appetite determines how much volatility you're comfortable with, while your time horizon reflects how long you can stay invested before you might need the money. Together, these factors govern which investment options would suit you best. Here are a few options:

Time Horizon	Risk Appetite		
	Low	Moderate	High
6 months to 1 year	• Savings account • Liquid fund • Arbitrage funds	• Savings account • Liquid fund • Arbitrage funds	• Savings account • Liquid fund • Arbitrage funds
Up to 2 years	• Fixed deposits • Short-term debt funds • Arbitrage funds	• Fixed deposits • Short-term debt funds • Arbitrage funds	• Fixed deposits • Short-term debt funds • Arbitrage funds

Time Horizon	Risk Appetite		
	Low	Moderate	High
Up to 3 years	• Fixed deposits • Short-term debt funds	• Equity savings funds	• Balanced advantage funds
3–5 years	• Fixed deposits • Equity savings funds	• Balanced advantage funds • Aggressive hybrid funds	• Diversified equity funds • Mid-cap funds • Small-cap funds
5–10 years and above	• Fixed deposits • Equity savings funds	• Diversified equity funds	• Diversified equity funds • Mid-cap funds • Small-cap funds

Evolution of Your Portfolio

Diwali has always been my favourite festival – the joy of diyas, sparklers and indulgent sweets. When I was growing up, it was a time for lavish family feasts, but over time, the plates grew lighter as healthy eating took precedence. The laddoos began to be moderated, the hearty lunches were swapped out for simpler dinners.

Your portfolio might follow a similar pattern. During your younger years, it might be tailored to handle a lot more risk with small-cap funds and high-growth bets. But mid-life might call for balance and your focus might shift to stability alongside growth, and you might prefer steady funds. As your retirement nears, it might be time to simplify your portfolio with more low-risk, steady options – like rejoicing in the comforting glow of diyas more than the indulgent festivities.

> **KEY LEARNINGS**
> - What dal-chawal is to a thali, your core portfolio is to your investments. Don't neglect the basics!
> - One hot stock won't make you rich, but one bad investment can set you back.
> - Your portfolio should evolve with you. What worked in your twenties may not suit you in your fifties. Keep an open mind and adjust to your shifting needs.

16

FINANCIAL TOOLS AND FEATURES

The SIP Family

Late at night, Raj Malhotra sat at his desk, clacking away on his typewriter. Writing had become his refuge after retirement – it gave him a sense of purpose and some income. He was immersed in deep creative thought when suddenly, his eldest son burst into the room, looking annoyed. 'Papa, can you stop this ruckus, please!? Unlike you, some of us have to go to work in the morning.'

Raj was flushed with embarrassment. 'I'm sorry,' he said.

The humiliation stung. Raj put away his papers and turned off his table lamp. Forced to live under his son's roof in his old age, he had no choice but to comply. Once the patriarch of the family, he had now been reduced to an unwelcome guest, his financial dependence stripping him of his dignity.

Millennials may recognize this is scene from *Baghban*

(2003), where Raj Malhotra (played by Amitabh Bachchan), a banker, devoted his life to his family only to be abandoned in his old age. Reliant on his sons taking care of him after retirement, he did not bother making any alternate plans. By the end of the movie, he had managed to write a bestselling novel that helped him regain his pride and financial independence.

Imagine if you were in this unfortunate situation (and it happens more frequently than we think) – how likely is it that you'll be able to write a bestselling book that pulls you out of your financial rut? Time for a reality check: 90 per cent of books in India sell fewer than 2,000 copies, so the odds aren't great. The odds of a well-planned investment portfolio securing your post-retirement life, on the other hand, are far better. Let us forget for a moment the irony of a banker not planning his own finances, and rewrite Raj Malhotra's story as a smarter man.

Regular Investing

What if Raj had planned for his retirement much before the day came? His bank job was both stable and reasonably paid. Let's say he started an SIP with just ₹10,000 a month during the early years of his career. As his salary grew, so did his SIP – he bumped it up by 10 per cent every year, turning it into a **step-up SIP**.

After a decade and a half of investing, the power of compounding kicked in. Raj's small, consistent investments had snowballed into something marvellous. By earning an average return of 12 per cent annually, here's what Raj ended up with on retirement, after investing for twenty-five years:

Year	Invested amount (₹)	Wealth Accumulated by Year-End (₹)
1	1,20,000	1,27,665
5	7,32,612	9,69,179
10	19,12,491	32,68,898
15	38,12,698	82,74,718
20	68,73,000	1,86,31,383
25	1,18,01,647	3,93,44,018

As you can see, Raj could have accumulated nearly ₹3.93 crore! Cherry on top: if he had also set up SIPs for specific goals, like creating a retirement corpus, planning occasional travel with his wife, Pooja, and his dream car, he could have achieved those too!

Some of you may also remember that in the movie, Raj had walked into a Mercedes Benz showroom and was humiliated by the salesman for taking the car out for a test-drive when he clearly couldn't afford it. Guess what? In our version of the plot, Raj's SIPs could actually have enabled him to buy the Benz of his dreams. Plus, he would not have needed his adopted son to turn rich and come to knock some sense into the rude salesman.

Like the reimagined Raj Malhotra, you can also consider using SIPs to invest. Here are some features of SIPs which set them apart as great financial products:

- **Step-up:** You can automatically increase your SIP amount every year by a fixed percentage or amount in proportion to the increase in your income.
- **Pauses:** If you can't afford to set money aside to put into your SIP for some time owing to a financial emergency of any sort, you can simply pause your investment without closing your SIP altogether. Contrary to popular opinion, an SIP is not like an EMI, where you have to pay the fixed amount every month or incur penalties if you can't manage that.
- **Value/Power SIPs:** These kinds of SIPs adjust monthly installments based on market conditions. They let you invest more when markets are down so that you accumulate more units at lower NAV.

A common misconception is that SIPs are a whole other financial product or asset class. Guess what? They are not. A SIP simply means investing a fixed amount at fixed intervals into mutual funds. I once overheard someone on a flight saying that they weren't investing in mutual funds, but 'in SIP'. I just rolled my eyes.

Rupee Cost Averaging

The funny thing is Raj Malhotra was not the only one of his kind. Why do you think so many people of his generation did not invest and get amazing returns, but rather preferred to remain glued to the safety of FDs? One reason could have been that they were probably afraid of the short-term volatility of equity. What if I told you that there exists a strategy by which you can deal with such volatility better?

It's called rupee cost averaging. Imagine you're at your favourite pizzeria, and instead of one big pizza, you get a slice every day for a month. Some days you buy it at the usual price, and on others, you might get it for a discount. Over time, however, the cost of your pizza cravings will average out. This is called rupee cost averaging, and this simple principle can be applied to mutual funds as well.

You may invest a fixed amount in a mutual fund at regular intervals, regardless of market conditions. When prices are high, you will get fewer units for the same amount; when prices are low, you will get more. Over time, this will average out the cost of your investments, reducing the overall impact of market volatility and doing away with the need to time the market.

Regular Cash Flow Needs

My mother-in-law has an unrelenting passion for travel. Even in her post-retirement years, she often jets off to explore new destinations, both domestic and international. Her love for experiencing new cultures, cuisines and landscapes has never wavered, and her friends are in awe of her active lifestyle.

'How do you manage it?' one of her friends once asked her. 'Your sons must be taking good care of you.'

My mother-in-law laughed, shaking her head. 'My sons don't fund my vacations. My SWP does.'

The room fell silent. Her friends exchanged curious glances. Traditionally, retirees relied on interest from their fixed deposits, or income from property rentals, or their pensions to foot their regular expenses. But now, times have changed. Until the 1990s, pensions were a common feature for both government and private-sector employees. Post-2005, however, with the introduction of the New Pension Scheme (NPS) and changing workplace policies, pensions became less common. But the need for a steady income after retirement is just as important today as it was back then.

My mother-in-law needed a sustainable way to fund her travel adventures and day-to-day expenses without draining her savings prematurely. That's why she spent a good portion of her earning years investing in hybrid mutual funds. When the corpus had grown to a sizeable sum, she started a Systematic Withdrawal Plan (SWP). So let's look at what an SWP even is.

An SWP allows investors to withdraw a fixed amount regularly from their mutual fund investments, while allowing the remaining amount to stay invested and grow. It's like creating your own pension scheme. For my mother-in-law, her SWP has been a means of financial strength. On the twenty-ninth day of every month, a fixed amount gets credited to her account from her corpus, just like a salary or pension. This reliable cash flow covers her travel and other expenses, giving her the freedom to pursue her passions without depending on anyone.

Making Your SWP Work for You

Imagine you have ₹50 lakh invested in a mutual fund. You decide to withdraw 6 per cent in a year (that's ₹3 lakh annually, or ₹25,000 a month) through an SWP, while the fund itself grows at 12 per cent per year. How much money do you think you'll have left in your mutual funds at the end of five years? Let's calculate:

Year	Starting Corpus (₹)	Withdrawal (₹)	Ending Corpus (₹)
1	50,00,000	3,00,000	52,83,838
2	52,83,838	3,00,000	56,01,736
3	56,01,736	3,00,000	59,57,781
4	59,57,781	3,00,000	63,56,553
5	63,56,553	3,00,000	68,03,177

Even after withdrawing ₹3,00,000 every year, your fund will still grow from ₹50 lakh to ₹68 lakh in five years! How? Well, the 6 per cent withdrawal rate will easily be covered up by the 12 per cent returns, so your fund will see year-on-year growth. The remaining amount will keep compounding, stacking return upon return. That's why your fund doesn't just stay steady – it grows bigger and better over time.

Benefits of SWP

- **Tax Efficiency**: Since only the gains on the withdrawn amount are taxable and not the entire amount, SWPs can be more tax-efficient compared to interest income from fixed deposits.
- **Capital Preservation and Growth**: By keeping the rest of your corpus invested, your portfolio grows over time, offsetting the impact of inflation and withdrawals.
- **Flexibility**: An SWP also allows you to adjust the withdrawal amount based on your changing financial needs over time, offering more control than rigid pension plans. You can increase or decrease your SWP amount any time.

As my mother-in-law often says: 'My SWP gives me the freedom to live my life on my own terms.'

Tip: SIPs build wealth, SWPs help you enjoy it ...

Familiar Sources of Income from Interest

Ravi, a soon-to-retire government employee, wanted to supplement his pension with income from interest. He had ₹12 lakh to invest. Instead of locking the entire

amount into a single long-term FD, he used a laddering strategy, splitting his money into FDs with staggered maturities:
- ₹3 lakh in a one-year FD
- ₹3 lakh in a two-year FD
- ₹3 lakh in a three-year FD
- ₹3 lakh in a four-year FD

Each year, one FD matured, giving Ravi steady cash flow for expenses or reinvestment. This approach ensured regular liquidity and let him benefit from changing interest rates. If the interest rate increased, Ravi had the opportunity to lock in his next maturing FD at the increased rate. And if it decreased, his other FDs were already locked in at the higher rate.

Laddering isn't limited to FDs; it works for Target Maturity Funds too. These low-risk debt funds invest in government bonds or PSU bonds, offering predictable returns, and stability for long-term goals.

Most of us in India instinctively reach for products which guarantee regular income. '*Paisa vaapis aana chahiye* (money should come back)' is a common sentiment, even if that means the overall returns on investments would be low; I learnt this in my early start up days at Forefront. What we don't realize is that recurring income doesn't have to come only from familiar interest-paying products. SWPs and laddering are smarter ways to achieving your goal of getting a regular income while keeping your larger corpus growing.

Emergency Funds

Anjali was excelling in her job as a marketing manager at a food delivery start-up. She was being recognized for her creative skills and her ability to deliver results. But then the global funding slowdown of 2022 hit, shaking up the start-up ecosystem, and her company, like many others, announced massive layoffs to cut costs. Anjali suddenly found herself unemployed.

While the situation was nerve-wracking, she wasn't panicking. Years ago, she had started building an emergency fund, carefully setting aside enough to cover twelve months of her expenses. This cushion became her lifeline during this period of uncertainty. She didn't need to feel pressured to leap at the first job that came her way – especially since many offered salaries far lower than her previous pay. Instead, she used this time to upskill, learning advanced marketing tools and strategies through online courses. She even completed a certification in digital analytics, a high-demand skill in her field. Six months later, Anjali landed a new role at a fast-growing tech company with a 25 per cent higher salary than her previous job.

'My emergency fund was my safety net during the unexpected free fall,' she said. 'It gave me the confidence to hold out for the right opportunity rather than settling for something substandard out of desperation.'

Let's see what tools helped Anjali tide through her crisis:

- **Savings account** for immediate access to small sums, covering day-to-day needs.
- **Liquid funds** or a backup reserve for the larger expenses, offering better returns than a savings account and quick accessibility.
- **Credit card** as a stopgap solution for immediate, high-cost needs, which she repaid at the earliest opportunity to avoid incurring high interest.

Anjali's story is proof that an emergency fund is paramount for making bold, empowered decisions, even in crisis. Think of financial tools like SWPs, SIPs, liquid funds and annuities as the beams and ropes holding up the bridge to your financial freedom. With clear goals and the right products, you'll be able to secure your future like a pro before you know it!

KEY LEARNINGS

- An SIP today can save you from financial stress tomorrow. Start small, but start now.
- Retirement isn't a fairy tale. Plan for it, or risk a *Baghban* fate.
- SWPs are like your personal ATMs, providing a steady cash flow from the wealth you accumulated over time.

17

MONEY HYGIENE

Clean Up to Cash In

My friend Dhana arrived in India. His face carried the weight of the many sleepless nights and the long flight from New Zealand he was not entirely prepared for. Dhana worked as a DevOps engineer for a software company in Auckland, when the news of his mother's sudden passing turned his world upside-down. He took the next available flight to India and immersed himself in the solemn rites and rituals.

Weeks passed before Dhana was able to find his feet again; it was almost time for him to return to New Zealand. There were still many matters to resolve – the most important thing on his list of tasks was accessing his mother's bank locker, which held the all-important property papers he would need to sell off their family home in due time. With his folder of required documents, he made his way to bank manager's desk. The manager was a middle-aged man with kind eyes, who ushered him into a small cabin to set the process in motion.

'I need to see the death certificate, please,' the manager said. 'And your identification documents.'

Dhana handed him the documents. The manager looked through them carefully, and then turned to his laptop. After clicking away for a few moments, he looked at Dhana with his brow furrowed. 'Mr Dhanasekharan,' he said, 'I'm sorry, but according to our records, your mother did not mention a nominee for her locker.'

The words struck Dhana like lightning. His mother had been very meticulous; the kind of person who kept every receipt of hers in labelled folders. The idea that she hadn't listed a nominee felt unthinkable, yet here he was.

The manager explained further, patiently but firmly, that the rule was clear: 'Legal heir(s) of the deceased locker hirer will be allowed to access the locker and remove the contents on producing duly certified copy of legal representation i.e. Probate of a Will or Letter of Administration or Succession certificate along with the copy of death certificate.'

In layman language, nothing could move forward without the due legal clearances. Dhana sat there in stunned silence, dreading at the labyrinth of bureaucracy he would have to brave to achieve this one crucial feat, but that he simply didn't have the time or energy for. The process could take months, or even years, depending on how things panned out. But he had no choice. So after several months and round trips between the two countries, Dhana finally managed to gain access to his mother's locker and the property documents. But all of this was a huge drain on him, emotionally.

The lesson was clear: something as simple as naming a nominee can save our loved ones from a lot of financial chaos in the future. And this does not just apply to nominations; passwords, documents, wills, etc. are important aspects of financial hygiene that may seem like annoyances to us, but tend to have a huge impact on the financial futures of our loved ones as well as our own. It is certainly worth striving for, and you can achieve it using my simple checklist mentioned below.

The Money Hygiene Checklist

Whether it's a sudden emergency or your dream opportunity, your money needs to be as on-point as you are. So, here's a checklist to keep your financial life neat and tidy:
- [ ] KYC
- [ ] Nominations
- [ ] Address updates
- [ ] Tax returns and receipts

KYC

When Amit needed money to pay his dad's hospital bills, he was stuck – his account was frozen because he had ignored the bank's emails about updating his Know Your Customer (KYC) records, so now he could not make any transactions. Ouch.

Don't make Amit's mistakes. KYC information is to help your bank know it's really you managing your money. This generally comprises proof of your identity (Aadhaar, PAN card, etc.) and your current address. These norms exist to prevent fraud and shady or illegal activity, like money laundering and terror financing. Skipping this crucial check could leave you locked out of your own account and unable to access your own money. Keep your KYC records updated with your financial institutions at all times.

Nominations

Remember what happened to Dhana? He could have avoided the hassle of jumping through hoops to access his mom's bank locker if only she had added him as her nominee. Think of nominations as treasure maps for your loved ones. If you don't mention these for all your assets and accounts, you'll leave them guessing the equivalent of 'open sesame' for the door to your wealth, and if by a miracle, they do figure out the magic words, without being named as your nominees, they won't be let in! Make sure you update your nominations after life events like deaths, marriage, divorce or kids. This will help you ensure that the right people can lay claim to the assets you leave behind.

Address Updates

Priya was living the high life in her new home when she realized she'd missed reminders about her FD maturing.

She did some digging, only to find out that her bank was still sending all communication to her old address. Her FD had auto-renewed at a lower rate before she could opt for a higher-interest alternative. Ugh. Always keep your home and email addresses up-to-date with your banks and investment accounts. Missed mail can turn into missed money pretty quickly.

Tax Returns and Receipts

Manish thought a late tax filing notice could hardly do any real harm. A year later, he found that the tax department had frozen his account. Manish's wallet wasn't amused at the penalty imposed on him, either. File your taxes on time, every time. Also remember to keep your receipts and returns safe for at least six years – audits have a way of showing up like cops to crash one hell of a party.

Tip: Your money should be easy to access, not trapped in paperwork.

Tracking Investments

Do you keep track of everything you own? Sounds like a no-brainer that it's good practice to do so, right? My uncle Nikhil, an old-school investor, bought stocks back in the days when 'shares' were actual paper certificates, not app icons on a screen. Over the years, he had collected shares like seashells on a seashore. With a mind-boggling 250 stocks, he had pretty much the entire index in his portfolio. He moved to the US for a work opportunity a few years later, leaving his stockpile at home.

Once day, his mother was on a cleaning spree when she stumbled upon a stack of dusty papers that were kept so meticulously, they were bound to be important. She called him up and said, 'I think I found your old stocks'. One of them was Nestlé, a name she recognized from the pantry. Little did his mother know she'd found a golden ticket. The stock had quietly ballooned into a fortune, and was now worth crores. Yes, crores.

Nikhil was floored by the discovery. That forgotten gem enabled him to return to India and live a nice, comfortable retirement. Imagine that! A retirement plan he didn't even remember setting up!

I remember a friend of mine calling me once, panicking at an outstanding amount on her late husband's credit card. Years after his passing, one of the several credit cards he owned was still active, and someone had used it for a fraudulent transaction. Lots of phone calls and paperwork later, we managed to close the account and restore her peace of mind. The entire painful ordeal could have been avoided if her husband had simply shared the details of his credit card account with her beforehand.

The truth is, people don't really know to be serious about tracking their investments and maintaining records of all their accounts. Back in the day, converting physical shares into digital format was not as easy as it is today. And when you own various assets like real estate, stocks, mutual funds and UTI bonds – it can be a daunting task to keep track. So how do you do it? Sure, there are apps for everything these days, but they may not provide the kind of meticulous, safe or comprehensive tracking required.

It is thus advisable that you create an investment tracker of your own to ensure that knowledge of your investments is shared with the people you wish to have benefit from it.

Investment Tracking Checklist

Tracking your investments might not sound fun, but it makes your money work harder for you. Whether it's an FD quietly renewing at a subpar rate, a mutual fund that's lost its spark, or a property tax you forgot to pay, small slip-ups can snowball into missed opportunities if left unattended for too long.

The good news is: staying on top of your portfolio doesn't have to be complicated. With a little organization and the right tools, you can manage all your assets with ease. Here's a simple guide to keeping your investments in check; one asset class at a time.

Fixed Deposits (FDs)

FDs are like that quiet friend who doesn't ask for constant attention. Log in to your netbanking account regularly to check interest rates and renewal dates. Keep an eye out for those reminder emails from your bank when an FD is close to maturity. Trust me, it's better than letting your FD just roll on into mediocrity for an eternity.

Real Estate

Keep your physical property documents safe and scan them for digital backups as well. Don't forget to do the same for tenant agreements – especially if you live in a rental. Why, you ask? Because digging for papers during a resale or if ever a legal issue arises can bring a lot of unnecessary stress.

Mutual Funds and Stocks

Mobile apps have now made it super easy to monitor your mutual funds and stocks. Stocks need attention because they're always up to something – dividends, corporate actions, price swings … there's way too much you don't want to miss out on. Link your demat account with a trading platform or app for regular updates. Subscribe to NSDL's CAS (Combined Account Statement) to get a bird's-eye view of your portfolio.

Insurance Policies

Dematerialize your policies with an e-insurance account (eIA) to make it easier to keep track of your premium schedules, policy numbers and renewal dates, either using apps or spreadsheets. Set reminders for your premiums to avoid lapses in coverage. Review policies annually to ensure they still meet your needs before it's time to pay your premium.

Gold and Precious Metals

For physical gold, store it safely and keep purchase invoices handy. For digital gold or ETFs, your brokerage platform has you covered. Update your records periodically with the purchase price and current market value if you are using offline tools. This way, you'll know exactly how shiny your investment is!

Loans and Liabilities

Loans are the grownup version of borrowing your friend's car. If you don't return it on time, the relationship can get awkward. Keep track of all your loans in any tracker of your choice, noting EMIs, interest rates and tenures.

Personal Financial Log

Your personal financial log is a document where you would jot down account details, policy numbers, maturity dates and even contact info for your bank or insurer. This should be stored securely and shared only with trusted family members or financial advisors. You never know when life might throw you the next curveball and this is an excellent way to be prepared.

We have included a sample personal financial log for you to download and use on the Mango Millionaire website. Remember to review and update this log regularly. Treat this as an act of love and responsibility towards your loved ones as it will not only protect them from unnecessary stress, but also ensure that your financial legacy remains well preserved.

KEY LEARNINGS

- Financial clutter is like a messy closet; easy to ignore until you're desperately searching for something important.
- Nominations are key to ensure your wealth lands in the right hands in that distant future.
- You track your steps, calories, and screen time. Use the same discipline to keep track of your finances.

18

MONEY BEHAVIOUR

Don't Follow the Herd, Lead the Pack

In Greek mythology, Daedalus – a brilliant craftsman – and his son Icarus, were trapped by the jealous King Minos on the island of Crete. To help them escape, Daedalus built wings using feathers and wax – a genius invention – but before they took flight, he warned Icarus, 'Fly steady. Too low, and the sea will ruin your wings. Too high, and the sun will melt them. Stay in the middle, where you'll be safe.'

At first, Icarus listened. He began soaring over the sea as the wind rushed past him. But soon, the thrill of flying got the better of him. *Why not go higher?* he thought. Ignoring his father's yells, Icarus flew toward the blazing sun and the wax in his wings melted, plunging him right into the sea.

While this story is a myth, it holds a valuable lesson relevant to all of us. Daedalus' intelligence created the perfect plan, but did not account for Icarus's behaviour, which was ultimately their undoing. In life – and especially in investing – everything depends on striking the right balance between your intelligence and your behaviour. It is your intelligence that will help you build your wings but only your behaviour will determine the fate of your flight. Even the best-crafted wings can fail if you don't break out of unhelpful behavioural patterns early on. This is one of the root causes of why so many investors lose money in the market. But what does the ideal investor behaviour look like? Let's take a closer look.

Don't Exit During the Interval

Two friends, Dominic and Zaheer, decided to try their luck in the stock market in December 2007. Both invested ₹10,000 each in a midcap mutual fund, purchasing 1,000 units at an NAV of ₹10. But then the 2008 global financial crisis hit. By March, the NAV nosedived to ₹3 – a shocking 70 per cent drop. Dominic couldn't take the heat and decided to move his money into a fixed deposit in panic. 'At least I'll have some peace of mind now,' he said.

But Zaheer remain unperturbed, 'In Bollywood movies, the villain may throw a few punches, but the hero always makes a comeback and wins.' He stayed invested. Fast forward to December 2024, Dominic's fixed deposit had grown at 7 per cent annually. Feeling smug, he called up Zaheer to boast about his earnings.

He was in for the shock of his life. The NAV of the midcap fund had skyrocketed to ₹100, and Zaheer's 1,000 units were now worth ₹1,00,000, boasting a stunning 10x growth and a 14.4 per cent annualized return (CAGR).

'How did you manage this blockbuster ending?' Dominic asked.

'I stayed to see what happens after the interval!'

And boy, was Zaheer right! Like we've said before, markets recover over time. This is a fact, especially in the Indian context. Over any ten-year period, the odds of the Nifty 50 delivering positive returns have been high due to India's consistent economic growth, the magic of compound interest and market corrections smoothing the graph out over time. But like any great film, you must wait for the climax to enjoy the full movie and not exit during the interval.

Moo to Boo: The Cost of Living Too Large

One day in sixteenth-century India, a farmer visited King Krishnadevaraya with an unusual request.

'Your Majesty, I have a cow that produces the richest milk in the kingdom. If I had a golden bell for her, she'd look truly royal as she deserves to.'

Amused, the king granted his wish. The farmer tied the golden bell around the cow's neck, but just as he turned to look back at his humble hut, he couldn't help but feel that it didn't quite match the cow's grandeur.

So he borrowed money to revamp his house. But then he looked down at his clothes and felt they didn't suit someone living in such a fine house, so he bought expensive new ones. Months later, the farmer returned to the palace, this time in tears.

'Your Majesty, I've lost everything! I spent all I had on the house, clothes and grand feasts. Now I can't even afford fodder for my poor cow.'

Just as the king began to feel regret at granting the man's foolish wish for the golden bell in the first place, his trusted and witty advisor Tenali Rama spoke. 'Maharaj, it is not the golden bell that ruined him. His own greed for a lifestyle he couldn't afford did. Instead of investing his wealth into improving his farm and steadily getting richer with the support of his prized cow, he got caught up in appearances and spent the little he had.'

This story is the perfect metaphor for what lifestyle inflation can look like – as income grows, so does the temptation to upgrade homes, gadgets, or take fancy vacations. But unchecked spending erodes potential wealth, leaving little for emergencies, or even long-term goals. So make your financial decisions to match your goals, not someone else's Instagram reels. Prioritize investing alongside the occasional indulgence.

Bloom to Bust

Back in seventeenth-century Netherlands, everyone from wealthy merchants to humble bakers was obsessed with buying tulips – not because they loved flowers, but because everyone around them was doing it. Rare bulbs were selling for the price of a house! Yes, a *house*! People believed the prices would just keep going up. And then, pop! The prices came crashing down when everyone realized, 'Wait, they are just flowers.'

Those who had bet their life savings on tulips just to keep up with the times were left clutching onto nothing but worthless bulbs and a whole lot of regret. This phenomenon, called 'Tulip Mania', is often cited as an example of herd mentality.

I see it, too, whenever I visit Delhi. It feels like the whole city is following the latest investment trend. One year, it's Bitcoin; the next year, it's small-cap funds. During the Bitcoin craze, I couldn't even sit down for dinner at any gathering without someone excitedly talking about how 'Everyone's buying Bitcoin! I just can't miss out!'

But guess what? FOMO (Fear of Missing Out) isn't a good investment strategy, no matter how thrilling it may seem. Don't jump onto the latest bandwagon just because everyone else is on it. It's tempting to go after what everyone else is having at your neighbour's cocktail party, but remember that trends come and go, and a good investment is meant to tide the times with you. It is supposed to help you grow your wealth long after the hype dies down.

Bad Shoes Are Like Bad Stocks: Walk Away

Imagine you had purchased a pair of shoes which don't fit as well as you hoped they would. Do you think it's wise to hold onto them, hoping they'll magically become comfortable someday? Of course not. Wouldn't you rather exchange them for shoes that actually fit? Similarly, in investing, people cling to losing stocks in the hope that they will someday rebound, even as better opportunities stare them in the face.

Remember the infra stock craze of 2007? Real estate and infrastructure IPOs had hit the market and attracted massive subscriptions. But soon, these stocks tanked and never recovered; even more than a decade later. If you have purchased a bad product, better to cut your losses than let hope drag you down further into the pit. Sometimes, the best move is to let go.

Hot Stocks and Cold Reality

From the mid to late '90s, the Internet was the new thing in India and Sify Broadband was riding that wave like a pro. In 1999, it became the first Indian internet company to be listed on NASDAQ. Its shares debuted at $18, and investors couldn't get enough.[1] Sify's stock price soared to incredible heights and everyone became convinced India was on the brink of an internet revolution.

But beneath all the hype, this excitement was fuelled more by **recency bias** rather than a solid understanding of how businesses work. Investors had completely ignored the reality of India's limited internet infrastructure at that time. By 2000, Sify's stock plummeted alongside its Western counterparts. Trillions of dollars evaporated. This story is an important reminder of why it's dangerous to focus only on what's hot right now. Such decisions are often driven by a potent mix of fear and greed. Greed arises due to unrealistic expectations. As of December 2024, midcap funds are posting impressive short-term numbers: one-year returns of 31 per cent and three-year returns of 22 per cent. But these are not the norm. The long-term average return for midcap funds sits closer to 15 per cent. That's the figure investors should keep in mind.

In March 2020, markets took a hit, with returns sinking into the red as the pandemic triggered a global crash. Yet, the three years that followed told a very different story, with markets bouncing back to deliver stellar returns. This is the perfect representation of the cyclical nature of investing. You can steer clear of recency bias by adopting a more thoughtful and disciplined approach:

- **Think long-term:** Evaluate an investment's performance over a horizon of five to ten years rather than focusing solely on recent returns, whether exceptionally high or low. A long-term perspective will help you look beyond short-term fluctuations and provide a clearer picture of its true potential.
- **Diversify:** Spread your investments across different

Asset Management Companies (AMCs) with varying investment styles such as a focus on growth, value and quality. Additionally, diversify your investments across asset classes – equity, debt, hybrid, international funds and gold – to reduce dependency on any single asset class and enhance your portfolio's resilience.

- **Dig deeper:** When a fund has delivered strong performance over the past couple of years, analyse the underlying factors driving its success. Is it a sectoral skew that is helping the outperformance, concentrated positions in a few stocks driving the returns, or the style of the fund manager which is working out well? Assess whether these factors are likely to persist in the long run. Keep in mind that extreme outperformance or underperformance often mean reverts, gradually aligning with long-term averages over time.

Tip: Emotions make for great stories but terrible investment strategies.

No Perfect Time

How many folks out there with a crystal ball foresaw the financial crash of 2008 or the 2020 pandemic? Certainly not too many. **Timing the market is a myth;** trying to guess the perfect moment to buy low and sell high is a futile effort. Markets are influenced by countless factors that no one can predict correctly consistently (not even the so-called experts).

Take 2020, for instance. The pandemic hit and by March, the markets had nosedived. Many investors sold off all their stocks, convinced the worst was yet to come. But then, surprise! By the end of the year, the market had bounced back in one of the fastest recoveries ever, powered by stimulus packages and newfound optimism. Those who bailed, missed out on the rebound as well as the unforeseen profits of the recovery wave.

Trying to outsmart short-term ups and downs often causes you to lose sight of the bigger picture. The better strategy is to stay invested. People always ask me, '*Kab invest karna hai?* (When should I invest?)'. But the right question is '*Kab tak invested rehna hai? (Until when should I stay invested?)*'.

Bullish Mistakes

Do you know when most investment mistakes happen? *Ding ding ding!* During bull runs! These upturns can make even the most cautious investors feel invincible. But what feels like a winning strategy during the boom often ends in regret when the *mandi* (downturn) hits. During bull runs, everything seems to be touching new highs and people feel encouraged to invest in even the most obscure assets (like a new cryptocurrency) in their search for quick riches. Instead, they are often hit with steep losses when the markets crash or stabilize.

Stay mindful of these behavioural tendencies, whether it's the temptation to hit the panic button at the first market dip, or spend every extra rupee you earn on indulgences. Your patience *will* be rewarded with something invaluable: peace of mind from knowing that you're in control of your financial future.

> **KEY LEARNINGS**
>
> - If you exit at the interval, you'll miss the blockbuster ending (returns).
> - A bad stock won't magically recover. Cut your losses and move on.
> - The only FOMO you should have is fear of missing out on long-term gains.

References

- 'Satyam Sizzles on NASDAQ debut', Telegraph India, 19 October 1999. Available at: https://www.telegraphindia.com/business/satyam-sizzles-on-nasdaq-debut/cid/911473.

19

FINANCIAL ADVICE

Because Google Isn't Enough

Monty the monkey was swinging past a construction site when he spotted a big log with an axe driven into it. The workers were on a lunch break so Monty leapt at the chance to test out his skills. After all, he had been observing the workers for days. If they could do it, why couldn't he?

'Hmm,' Monty said, inspecting the axe. 'What's this? Some kind of fancy stick?'

Grinning mischievously, he tugged at it. Nothing happened. He used all his strength and managed to yank it loose. With a loud crash, the two halves of the log slammed shut and the force sent birds flying out of the trees. Poor Monty screamed as his tail got caught between the halves. He hopped around, shrieking and waving his arms, but was unable to wriggle free. The workers returned to find Monty stuck, regret painted all over his face. They quickly released him and sent him on his way with some sound advice: 'Next time, Monty, better leave the carpentry to the carpenters!'

Monty's approach to the carpenter's axe isn't all that different from how many of us approach our finances. We try to fix things ourselves without fully understanding the risks and then wind up in situations we can't easily escape from. I hear these stories all the time, even in my own extended family.

Mutual Funds and Mutual Regrets

One day, a cousin of mine called me out of the blue. Her voice, usually cheerful, was shaky and nervous because her finances were a mess. For the past two years, she had been on the mutual fund and stock market bandwagon, but instead of building a solid, diversified portfolio, she had poured nearly all her savings into banking-, international- and manufacturing-themed funds, which were top performers at the time when she was starting out. But the subsequent downturn in some of these sectors had wreaked havoc in her portfolio. Her overall portfolio was negative even when the broader market was positive.

'Did you consult a financial advisor before investing?' I asked her.

'No ... I didn't know where to start. It seemed too expensive a hassle.'

I sighed. 'The cost of seeking that advice would've been far less than what you've already lost by now.'

A financial planner would have diversified her portfolio and mitigated the risks she hadn't been able to foresee. Over the next few weeks, we decided to work on putting her financial life back on track. It began with one simple lesson: 'Good financial advice isn't an expense but an investment into avoiding costly mistakes later.'

Beach Bliss to Financial Miss

Do you dream of an early retirement? Oh come on, who doesn't? FIRE (Financially Independent, Retired Early) is all the rage! Sipping coconut water on a sunny beach at forty-five years of age with no risk of Monday blues anymore ... it all sounds so perfect. But eight out of ten people chasing this dream have no idea how much money they'll even need for a peaceful retirement. Ask a millennial about their investment goal and you'll most likely hear 'I'm saving for the future'.

Then there are mutual fund beginners who invest based solely on past performance. And let's not forget traders with beginner's luck. Doubling ₹10,000 in F&O might feel like a masterstroke, but it often leads to overconfidence and in time, messy losses. So why do so many investors make these very mistakes? There are three key reasons:

- **Time vs. Expertise:** Many think investing is as simple as choosing a few funds or stocks and watching them grow. True investing goes far beyond that. You need a holistic financial strategy tailored to meet your goals and circumstances. Unfortunately, most people are too busy juggling work, family and the rest of their lives to research and design such a strategy successfully for themselves.

- **Complexity of Goals:** Financial goals aren't one-dimensional. Buying a house, saving for a child's education, planning your retirement – they all have different timelines, risks and investment needs. While many people chase the 'best-performing fund', the smarter move is to find the one that aligns closely with your goals. A fund delivering short-term gains might not work for someone saving for the next twenty years.
- **Self-awareness:** Risk appetites vary widely and one's financial needs evolve over time. High-risk, high-reward strategies that incite excitement today might terrify you after a decade. A trusted financial advisor can help you navigate these shifts adeptly and manage your investments suitably.

Decoding Financial Experts

My cousin had tried a DIY approach because she didn't know where to start her financial planning. 'How do you even know who's the right person to approach?' she had asked.

She wasn't wrong to be anxious and doubtful. The world of financial intermediaries can be a real maze for someone to navigate when they are entirely unfamiliar with the financial world and its jargon. I decided to help her look for professionals who could help her out. A financial advisor is like a co-pilot for your financial journey. Not all advisors are created equal and the wrong choice can lead to unnecessary risks or suboptimal results, so a lot hinges on this seemingly simple choice.

'Start by checking their credentials,' I told her. 'Look for SEBI-Registered Investment Advisor (RIA) certification for advisors and an Association of Mutual Funds in India (AMFI) certification for mutual fund distributors (MFDs). They are reliable indicators that the professional or institution is qualified to provide financial advice and adheres to ethical standards.'

An RIA is a financial professional authorized by SEBI to provide investment advice. AMFI regulates mutual fund distributors and ensures that they comply with the necessary ethical practices in place for selling mutual funds.

When it comes to managing your money, you can go with big institutions like banks or wealth firms, or opt for individual MFDs and RIAs. For personal touch, that is someone who knows your financial story like a trusted family doctor would know your medical history, an individual advisor or a mutual fund distributor might be the way to go for you. If you value the credibility of a big institution, you might lean toward banks or wealth firms. While your relationship manager at these places might change, the institution continues to stand. Ultimately, it all boils down to your personal choice and comfort. Here's a snapshot of what distinguishes the two types of professionals:

Aspect	Mutual Fund Distributor	Registered Investment Advisor
Scope	Selection and execution of mutual funds	Assistance with all financial products from stocks, F&O to mutual funds
Approach	<ul><li>Recommendations based on investment objectives</li><li>Mutual fund portfolio creation</li></ul>	Goal- and risk-specific planning
Compensation	Brokerage paid by the mutual fund company	Fees paid by investor
Ideal For	Creating mutual fund portfolio and executing transactions therein	<ul><li>Goal-based planning</li><li>Tax and estate planning</li><li>Stock recommendations</li></ul>
Regulation	AMFI-registered	SEBI-registered

'What about fees?' she asked.

'A good professional will explain their fee structure upfront,' I said. 'If they dodge the question or push products with promises of "guaranteed returns", that's a red flag. Turn around and run away as fast as you can.'

Armed with this checklist, she began her search. After talking to a few candidates, she found a planner, advisor and distributor who checked all the boxes.

Checklist

- ☐ Check for your advisor's RIA or your MFD's AMFI certification
- ☐ Ask about the fees structure
- ☐ Beware of phrases such as 'guaranteed returns' and question-dodging
- ☐ Ensure transparency and clear communication
- ☐ Do you trust this individual/institution?
- ☐ Read all terms and conditions carefully before investing

Quarterly Reviews, Lifetime Gains

Hiring professionals was just the first step. I then started helping my cousin understand the importance of regular review meetings with her financial advisor to track progress and adjust strategies based on changes in her life or in the market. 'Please be completely honest during these reviews,' I warned her, 'whether it's debts, expenses, expectations or fears, share freely with your advisor. Professionals can't help you if you don't give them the full picture.'

She was nervous about meeting her advisor. I spent a lot of time talking to her and helping her define clear financial goals for herself: paying off loans, saving for milestones and long-term planning. This calmed her a bit.

Next, we built a quarterly review framework to keep her with the reviews:

- **Fixed Dates:** Set up pre-scheduled reviews every three months.
- **Preparation:** Make a list of questions and updates for your advisor beforehand to make the most of these meetings.
- **Tracking Progress:** Maintain a simple tracker on your own to keep an eye on your milestones.
- **Flexibility:** Adjust your plans after life changes, like job shifts or emergencies.

By her third quarterly review, my cousin felt confident, prepared and proactive. Her bond with her advisor was built on trust and had become a cornerstone of her financial journey. She finally had a professional in her corner who was ensuring her finances successfully tided the times with her through all her life's challenges.

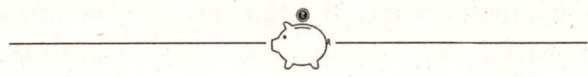

Tip: You don't need to get rich to seek professional financial advice, but to stay rich, you need advice.

When Not to Self-medicate

In the digital age, the Internet is ever-present to offer all kinds of advice. There are several portfolio trackers and DIY financial tools – free information that's just a click away. It is certainly tempting to skip paying for professional guidance and believe you have it handled. After all, why would you hire an advisor to tell you where to invest when Google can do it for free?

But think about this: would you trust Google over a doctor to treat a serious illness? Self-medicating based on online advice might still work for something like a minor headache (although we wouldn't recommend that either), but for something complex, wouldn't you feel more confident consulting a doctor to avoid making things worse?

Well, your financial health deserves the same level of care. Consider this: with a portfolio worth ₹5 crore, hiring an advisor might cost you 1 per cent annually, i.e. ₹5 lakh or approximately ₹41,000 a month. It might still feel like a lot and seem wholly avoidable, but the dangers of investing without technical knowhow far outweigh the pleasures. A single mistake, like investing in the wrong product, overexposing your portfolio to risk, or even misjudging market trends could cost you massive amount of money in lost returns. So choose wisely!

Tip: Sound advice for a nominal fee is an investment, not an expense.

The Curious Case of Missing Investors

I was once invited to give a talk at a Management Development Programme (MDP) in Goa. The auditorium was packed with senior working professionals. When I went on the stage, I opened with a simple question: 'How many of you know what mutual funds are?'

Nearly every hand shot up.

'Great! And how many of you actually invest in mutual funds?'

90 per cent of these hands went down! Curious, I asked the participants why they weren't investing despite knowing about mutual funds. The answers came quickly: 'We don't know how to get started'; 'It seems complicated'; 'Isn't it risky?'

Their hesitation wasn't surprising. The idea of managing money can feel overwhelming when you're just starting out. But there's plenty of help available, from financial advisors to investment platforms that can simplify the process.

Remember: financial success is rarely a solo act. Even the best investors have someone creating strategies and covering the blind spots for them. A good advisor or

MFD can equip you with two great tools to navigate the market: confidence and clarity. These are absolutely essential to set you on the path to financial freedom.

> **KEY LEARNINGS**
>
> - DIY can backfire in finance. One wrong move can cost you much more than expert advice ever will.
> - Following trends won't save you. Chasing past winners (hot stocks, best-performing funds) without a plan is like betting on yesterday's lottery numbers.
> - Good advice pays for itself. A trusted financial advisor or MFD is an insurance against costly mistakes and missed opportunities.

20

THE ECONOMY AND MONEY

The Kite and the Wind

On a sunny morning in Mumbai, Swapnil squeezed himself into the packed local train for his commute to Churchgate. Fresh out of hotel management school, he'd been hired as a trainee at a top hotel. His first paycheck was merely days away, and he was already excitedly dreaming about his new life with a two-wheeler. He'd buy it on a loan and bid goodbye to the crowded local train forever! He returned to the rattling compartment where he stood. A conversation between two other passengers suddenly caught his attention.

'Loans are going to get costlier,' one of them was saying. 'The RBI is going to hike repo rates.'

'Did you see the fiscal deficit last quarter?' The other responded. 'Growth *will* take a hit.'

Swapnil had no idea what they were talking about. He'd bunked most of his economics lectures in junior college to go watch movies at the nearby cinemas.

Terms like 'repo rates' and 'fiscal deficit' sounded vaguely familiar, but the mention of 'loans' was hard to ignore since it was directly relevant to his life. As the train approached its destination, Swapnil decided he needed to increase his financial awareness to understand how the economy could affect his life – his purchases, paychecks and even the job he had just started depended on it more than he'd realized.

As you'd have figured by now, mastering your finances doesn't require Swapnil – or you – to be a genius economist. However, a total lack of financial awareness can leave one feeling overwhelmed. But fear not, this chapter simplifies some of the key concepts you need to help you set more realistic expectations for your investments and steer clear of the fear mongering and other traps.

Global Economics = Local Headaches

Ishaan, a first-generation businessman, paced around his gourmet food store, the half-stocked shelves of chocolates and olive oils gleaming under the lights. A port strike in Europe had delayed his shipments, leaving him with empty shelves and frustrated customers – a storm he hadn't seen coming within the first month of him going into business. Neha, his friend who was a journalist at a trade magazine, stepped into the store just then.

'One strike at a port I've never even heard of,' Ishaan

said, 'and my store already feels like a sinking ship.'

'That's how interconnected everything is,' Neha said.

'But what can I possibly do?'

'Well, if you understand the connections of various factors that affect your business, you will be better prepared to deal with different situations. Let me explain. Think of your store as a country. Every good or service you produce adds to the country's economy. The sum total of all the sales you make comprise its gross domestic product or GDP.'

'Okay. So where are the suppliers in all this?'

'Somewhere near the top. Every time they raise their prices, the impact of it trickles down to all levels of the chain. That's inflation. The more you pay to your suppliers, the more you will need your customers to pay for your goods or services.'

'But what if they stop buying from me due to the rise in costs?'

'Then it can lead to slowdown in demand, and if this happens to many such businesses in one go, then your country can experience demand slowdown due to the rising prices, also called known as stagflation in the economy.'

'Right. Since demand is low, I can't even make up for the recurring cost of my shop and pay salaries of my staff, and I can't even ask for a short-term loan just to tide over this mess. Have you seen the interest rates lately?'

'High interest rates are part of the cycle. Central

banks raise them to cool down inflation by discouraging borrowing and reducing the cascading effects of inflation spreading to other parts of the economy.'

'So every time the global situation changes, you're telling me my "country" is likely to suffer a massive slowdown?'

'Well, if you're entirely at the mercy of global economic stability, then yes. But there's always room to adapt and future-proof your little country. You could diversify your sources of supplies. For your store, while local options might not be able to fully replace imports, but including enough of them can help you continue making money while the larger problem resolves itself. Which is why understanding economics is so helpful – it lends you a kind of foresight so you can be anticipate the impact of certain events on your business and prepare accordingly.'

Ishaan thanked Neha for her wisdom. She reminded him that things are not that simple, which is why there is no one way to deal with all kinds of economic developments. The only thing one can do is equip themselves with enough knowledge to know when it is time to adapt.

Over the next few weeks, the supply situation normalized and Ishaan's shop acquired adequate supplies to cater to the customers, who came flocking back in search of their favourite gourmet goods.

Tip: A slowing economy isn't the end, it's a reset. Stay invested.

The Amazing Indian Economic Ferris Wheel

Neha started dropping by Ishaan's shop more often just to see how he was doing and how learning about the global economics was going for him. They had a series of insightful conversations on the subject and Ishaan slowly began to see how the ebbs and flows of his business mirrored the larger economic cycles. He decided to put his newfound knowledge to use by investing his shop's earnings wisely and seeking Neha's counsel from time to time. 'Remember,' she told him, 'just like every seat on a Ferris wheel has to go the full circle, every business also has to ride waves of the economy and investment cycle. We can weather the ups and downs together.'

One afternoon, Ishaan was busy stocking his shelves when Neha walked in. He happily pointed her attention to the steady stream of customers. His workers were milling around as the wedding season had all customers buying in bulk. Business was thriving and the economy was booming. Neha nodded. 'We are going through an **expansion** phase, you see. Hence, your shop is teeming with customers. Enjoy it!'

She told him how 2021–24 was similarly a good

period for the Indian economy. India's GDP grew by 8.2 per cent in FY 2024, driven by increased consumer demand and post-pandemic market recovery. Everyone was investing in stocks and real estate and it was a great time to do so. Encouraged by this, Ishaan resolved to start investing in these two asset classes since they perform so well during growth periods.

Months later, during Diwali, Ishaan's shop was busier than ever. Yet, as he was updating his books one evening, he couldn't help but notice that things were starting to get expensive – suppliers had raised their prices and profits weren't growing as much as he'd hoped. He shared his concerns with Neha the next time she came by. She explained, 'This is the **peak**. The economy is running hot, but costs are rising.'

She described how in 2008, when stocks crashed during the global financial crisis, people lost their jobs but the value of gold remained steady. Taking her advice, Ishaan parked some of his earnings in gold and fixed deposits too. It was a safe move. For his shop, he decided to focus only on the essentials during uncertain times.

After Diwali, things slowed down. Customers visited less often, and unsold stocks began to accumulate. Ishaan sighed. 'It feels like the party's over.'

Neha had a different opinion. 'Far from it, my friend. This is the **contraction** phase,' she said. 'Businesses scale back, demand dips and everyone adjusts. But these times call for stability.'

Taking her advice, Ishaan turned to investing in bonds and fixed-income investments, which provided predictable returns during uncertain periods.

Next came the quietest months of the year. Sales were at their lowest, and Ishaan had to slash prices to clear old stock. He looked at Neha for an explanation again. 'This is the **trough**,' she said. 'And it's the best time to invest for growth.'

She reminded him how, after the slowdown from the COVID-19 pandemic, Indian equities rebounded dramatically as the economy recovered. She encouraged Ishaan to invest in stocks and real estate, betting on the next upswing, 'Rock bottom is where new beginnings lie.'

How to Apply Economics to Your Investments

Recognizing economic cycles and interconnections is the first step to making smarter, more informed investing decisions. Here are some practical steps to use the knowledge of the wider context to navigate financial uncertainties in your own life and seize opportunities with confidence.

- **Setting Expectations:** Economic indicators like inflation, interest rates and GDP help you gauge what the realistic returns on your investments will be during a certain period. FD returns hinge on interest rates, while stock market returns vary with economic growth and inflation. Over thirty years, India's stock market has delivered 13–14 per cent annualized returns, mirroring economic trends. Anything beyond that is a bonus. However, these returns don't remain consistent every year; some years returns can be negative and some years they can be positive.

- **Diversify:** Stocks thrive in growth phases, while bonds and gold provide stability during downturns. Balancing these assets in the right proportion ensures smoother sailing through economic cycles. Time your investments in each asset class accordingly.
- **Think Long Term:** Economic cycles are a reality. Ignore short-term noise and focus on the big picture. In a growing economy, think in terms of decades, not days. Even a bond fund might dip briefly, don't panic and stay the course.

A slowing economy isn't the end, it's a reset. Stay invested.

India's GDP showed growth by 8.2 per cent in FY 2024, and the economy is projected to grow at 6.5 per cent over the next two financial years, according to World Bank.[1] However, global events like wars and changing interest rate trajectories in other parts of the world can influence our GDP growth numbers. As long-term investors with basic financial awareness, we can leverage India's strengths to our advantage – a young population, a rising middle class and the digital revolution.

> **KEY LEARNINGS**
>
> - Inflation, interest rates and GDP directly impact your salary, loans and investments.
> - Stocks for booms; gold for uncertainty; bonds for downturns.
> - Markets rise, fall and rise again. Those who stay the course reap the rewards.

References

- 'Indian economy to grow at 6.7% for next two financial years, says World Bank', *Scroll*, 17 January 2025. Available at: https://scroll.in/latest/1078055/indian-economy-to-grow-at-6-7-for-next-two-financial-years-says-world-bank.

21

MONEY AND FAMILY

Little Lessons to Big Legacies

Raj and Priya's love story had all the makings of a fairytale. He was a charismatic entrepreneur; she a graceful homemaker. They got married and started their new life together with hope and enthusiasm. Their romance seemed eternal ... well, almost.

Unexpectedly, Raj's business took a downturn. The mounting financial pressure began to chip away at his cheer and unable to watch him get crushed under the burden, Priya reached out to an old friend of theirs for help. Her intentions were noble, but she could not have anticipated the consequences of her actions. Raj was furious when he discovered what she had done. 'Do you think I can't manage this on my own?' he yelled.

In the argument that followed, they both ended up saying hurtful things they couldn't take back. When the room finally fell silent, the air was heavy with their words. Their love, once so full of promises and dreams, was now strained by the financial stress.

This pivotal point in *Chalte Chalte* (2003), starring Shah Rukh Khan and Rani Mukherjee, is a classic example of how financial anxiety can wreak havoc on one's own peace of mind as well as that of their family's. Although the movie ends on a happy note, there are far too many families and relationships that have not been able to survive such testing times. Building a strong financial foundation, therefore, is also important for ensuring that our relationships can withstand such challenges.

This also reminds me of a dialogue from Emraan Hashmi's *Jannat*, a film about the high-stakes world of cricket betting and how greed can lead to one's downfall: '*Gareebi jab darwaze se andar aati hai na, toh pyaar khidki se bahar nikal jaata hai* (When poverty comes knocking at your door, love goes out the window)'.

A Family That Budgets Together Stays Together

Meet the Sahnis – Vivaan, Charul and their son, Aarav. Every evening, their dinner table was filled with lively debates about cricket, Bollywood gossip and the latest twists in their favourite family drama. But they never spoke about money – it was not because they were struggling financially or anything. Vivaan, an interior designer, and Charul, a management executive, earned good salaries. Yet, their savings often felt insufficient and they made their own financial decisions in silos, without any clear family-oriented strategy.

One evening, Aarav decided to change things, 'Why don't we discuss our money the same way we discuss everything else?'

While his parents were initially a bit hesitant, they eventually came around when they realized it would be good for all of them to talk about money openly. After all, if ever there was a crisis, they would all be in it together. The first thing they did was set shared financial goals. Buying a bigger home, planning an annual vacation and Aarav's education were top priorities. But before they invested their money, they needed to understand all of their risk appetites, liquidity needs and liabilities. Vivaan preferred high-risk, high-return investments, while Charul liked stability. Finding middle ground was crucial.

Next, they built a wealth plan. They diversified their investments across equities, real estate, fixed deposits and gold to balance risk and returns. They classified their investments into short term – for emergency funds and annual vacations – medium term – for a home down payment and car upgrade – and long term – for retirement and their child's further education. They tracked their liabilities closely, like their home loan instalments and monthly expenses, to ensure they never went off track. Charul and Vivaan made sure they had named nominees for all their holdings and assets, so Aarav never had to worry about anything in the future.

The Sahnis got into the habit of reviewing their finances every quarter, tracking their expenses, investments and savings using a simple spreadsheet. They adjusted their plan when needed, ensuring they remained on course. By being willing to talk about money more openly at home, the Sahnis built their financial awareness and discipline, and laid the foundations for well-managed generational wealth, one dinner conversation at a time.

From Piggy Banks to Portfolios

Aarav's first lesson in money management came when he was six years old. One day, Charul handed him a shiny blue piggy bank. At that age, money was just a piece of paper or metal that his parents exchanged for ice cream or his favourite comic books. He did not quite understand how it worked.

'This is your treasure chest,' Charul said with a smile as she handed the piggy bank to him. 'Handle it well.'

The clink of coins brought the child great joy and excitement. He used it to learn the joy of saving for small things, like a cricket bat or a toy car. When he turned ten, Vivaan and Charul took him to the bank to open his first savings account. Watching the clerk hand him a passbook with his name on it was such a thrill! Aarav knew just what to do with it and religiously deposited his birthday money and piggy bank savings into his account.

By the time he turned thirteen, he noticed that his parents would set aside some money every month. Curious, he asked them why and Charul explained,

'This is an SIP for your education. By the time you are ready to go to college, this money will have grown and will help you achieve your dreams.'

Vivaan and Charul had grown up in a very different India, where every rupee was stretched and financial security was not guaranteed. Saving for a rainy day wasn't optional – it was a way of life. As members of Generation X, they had been raised with the SST mindset of 'sasta, sundar, tikau', where affordability, durability and value for money are above all. Aarav, on the other hand, was part of Generation Alpha, and was growing up in a more prosperous India, where opportunities were abundant and lifestyles had completely changed. The common perception was that Generation Alpha did not value money the same way their parents did, so Vivaan and Charul took special care to ensure Aarav understood its value and did not take it for granted.

Years later, Aarav received his college acceptance letter from a prestigious university abroad. He was overjoyed but also worried if they could afford it. 'Dad, how will we manage to pay the fees?' he asked.

'Remember that SIP we started?' Vivaan said. 'That is what this is for.'

He showed his son how their investment had grown, helping him realize the importance of planning and patience. Their disciplined efforts had allowed him to study at one of the world's most prestigious universities, which had once seemed out of reach because of its sky-high fees.

Eventually, Aarav graduated with honours, and soon landed a job at a reputed firm. The excitement of his first paycheck was unmatched. But unlike many of his peers who were unsure of how to wisely manage their earnings, Aarav was already well-equipped. The financial lessons he had absorbed over the years from his parents had given him great clarity. When his first salary hit his bank account, Vivaan and Charul helped him set up his own SIP.

'This is your grown-up piggy bank,' Charul said, beaming with pride.

Aarav smiled at being able to uphold tradition. What his parents had started, he would now carry forward – not just for himself but for his family in the future. A strong foundation in money management ensures that when children become adults and start earning incomes, they know how to save, invest and plan their expenses so they never run out of money. For parents who worry that their children may not value money as much as they ought to, the best solution is the simplest. Talk about it. The lessons you teach your child today will help them fund their dreams tomorrow.

Tip: Money habits are inherited – make sure you pass on the right ones to the next generation.

The Thumbprint That Wasn't

In many films and serials, a lot of drama stems from matters of inheritance. Several years ago, an advertisement for the adhesive sealant M-seal became quite popular for its dark humour. It opened with an elderly man on his deathbed, looking frail, his son – his greedy *waaris* (heir) – hovering over him. Instead of comforting his father, the son had his eyes on the prize: the family fortune.

He hastily grabs a piece of paper – presumably a will he'd forged – and forcibly presses his father's thumb onto it for an impression. He smirks, thinking he's successfully pulled off his little stunt, but karma is quick to correct. A few drops of water drip from the ceiling and land right onto the precious thumbprint. The son then laments the failure of his devious attempt, completely ignoring his father who has finally passed away in the background!

Comical but grim, this ad leads us to a crucial subject: your will. A legally binding document clearly stating how you want your assets to be managed by someone after you're gone is absolutely essential. Here's why:

- **Avoids Disputes:** Clear instructions reduce misunderstandings and conflicts among heirs.
- **Respects Your Wishes:** Without a will, local inheritance laws govern what happens to which asset, and it may not align with your hopes and wishes.
- **Eases the Process:** Simplifies asset transfer, reducing the stress for your loved ones.

- **Provides for Dependents:** Secures the needs of minors, elderly family members and other dependents.
- **Enables Charity:** You can include any donations you'd like to make toward causes close to your heart.

The Effective Will Checklist

- ☐ List assets and assign beneficiaries
- ☐ Choose an executor to manage your estate
- ☐ Specify guardians for minors, if needed
- ☐ Update regularly to reflect any life changes
- ☐ Consult a professional to ensure legal compliance

Passing the Baton Without Dropping It

Building a legacy is all about ensuring it is managed with care even when you are no longer around to do it yourself. A well-thought-out plan can prevent misunderstandings, provide security and reflect your and your family's values more truly. Maintain a record of all your assets, including properties, investments and valuables, and share it only with trusted family members to avoid any confusion. Make sure you discuss your financial plans openly, especially with adult children, to ensure clarity and alignment on their part. If you have a child with special needs, set up a trust to ensure lifelong security for them with the help of financial planners, estate lawyers or special needs advisors.

Your Legacy Beyond Your Wealth

More than the wealth you build, a true legacy includes all the lessons you pass down – financial or otherwise. Families navigate life's journey together no matter how close or far apart they might live. As we draw to a close, I am reminded of Sooraj Barjatya's *Hum Saath Saath Hain* (1999), one of the most beloved family dramas in Indian cinema. And for good reason! The family at the centre of the movie goes from wealth to ruin and eventually recovers in a joyous ending. A family that eats together, stays together – and a family that transparently talks about money thrives together.

So good luck, dear reader! May your portfolios be diversified, your expenses be low and your generational wealth as secure as the family bonds in a Sooraj Barjatya film.

KEY LEARNINGS

- Talk money, avoid the mess. Openly discussing finances keeps families secure and stress-free.
- Teach them young. Kids who learn about money early on handle wealth wisely as adults.
- Wealth without a will inevitably ends in chaos.

AFTERWORD

The End and the Beginning

So you're done reading this book, congratulations! How do you feel? Confused by all the information? A little more informed about the world of money? Excited to start your investing journey? Most importantly, do you feel ready? Ready to make your first investment, set up your first SIP, buy your first stock – or at the very least, write down your money goals? We hope you are, because what is financial literacy worth if it is not applied? We believe in you – you got this!

Reading this book may have been quite a journey for you – sometimes, it may have felt hopeful and encouraging, but at other times, you may have struggled to accept, confront and be objective about your financial habits. As finance professionals, even though we live and breathe finance, writing it felt very similar. It was as much of a challenge as a pleasure. Distilling our years of knowledge and experience to simplify fundamental concepts for mango people wasn't easy. Finding the right words, cultural references and analogies to convey these deceptively complex ideas was an experience in itself. We learned so much – people's financial habits, stories and beliefs often left us inspired, but sometimes, they also made us feel pained and unsettled. All stories, however, reinforced one simple truth: money isn't just about numbers; it's about the life choices we make. Good money management isn't about talking stocks or sitting in front of a trading screen like in *The Wolf of Wall Street* (2013) – it is about good habits, knowing your goals and personality, and applying simple principles consistently. This book was written to help you view personal finance in a new light; to make it real, relatable and hopefully, a little less intimidating.

Remember

- **Don't be afraid of money.** Most financial stress comes from avoiding decision-making. The more you learn about money, the more in control of it you will feel.
- **This book is your friend, not a textbook.** Whether it's insurance, loans or investing, do not hesitate to go back to the relevant chapters whenever you need them. You don't have to remember everything you've read – you simply have to remember to return here to find it.
- **Making mistakes is part of the process.** No one gets it right from day one, and that's okay. What matters is that you learn and keep improving. Start small, make mistakes, get better and dive deeper.

- **The worst financial decision is doing nothing out of fear.** And the best decision is to start, no matter how small.

Finally, a little request from us. Financial literacy is a gift that keeps on giving – it can uplift individuals, families, communities and even entire nations. If you liked what you read and found it to be even a little useful, consider gifting a copy to someone you think will benefit from it. This ripple of inclusion and empowerment, my friends, will be our greatest reward as authors.

ACKNOWLEDGEMENTS

Writing a book can be so deeply personal, yet it takes a village to make it come alive. We are extremely grateful to everybody who made *Mango Millionaire* possible.

First and foremost, our heartfelt thanks to the entire team at Pan Macmillan India for believing in this idea and bringing it to the market. Pujitha, Udyotna and Isha – thank you. To our writing partners, Kashif, Michelle and the team at Bound India, it was a pleasure to collaborate with you on this project. Thank you for your patience, creativity and diligence during this process.

The original seeds of this book were sown by Rashesh Shah, who urged us to write a book on personal finance for India. Thank you Rashesh for encouraging us to push the boundaries again and again.

To our colleagues at Edelweiss Mutual Fund – thank you. The work you do, your insights, experiences and stories have shaped much of this book. The mutual fund industry and its commitment to educating and empowering ordinary Indians, and even succeeding in doing so every day at such a large scale, constantly inspires us. A special thanks to our army of financial intermediaries – mutual fund distributors and investment advisors – we know how hard you work to improve the financial lives of crores of investors. And to our investors – thank you for sharing your questions and experiences, which have helped us keep the book grounded in practical wisdom.

Finally, sincere thanks to our families. Making a book happen is about sacrificing weekends, working late nights, and missing family trips. Thank you for bearing with us through it all.

Radhika

Much of what we know about money is shaped by the people around us. Thank you to Mom for teaching me about financial independence as a young woman, and the importance of recognizing the value of money and the simple tenet of 'sasta, sundar, tikau'. Thank you to Papa for teaching me to make the big money decisions in life wisely, including my education, having a vision, setting goals, and finding balance. And thank you to my brother Anubhav for teaching me that money is also meant to be enjoyed! To my husband Nalin: thank you for being my partner on our money journey, building a beautiful life together and achieving our shared goals through sensible planning – and for making the best spreadsheets! Finally, to my little Remy, who already has SIPs of his own and is collecting coins in his piggy bank. Mama took away from your time with her – all those Sunday calls, on some of which you popped into view. Thank you, my little investor, for being so patient with her through it all.

Niranjan

Very early on, I learned something truly important about money – you can master it only if you genuinely respect it. Thank you, Mom, for teaching me this – my first real money lesson. Thank you for investing everything you had into giving me the right education, which built the strong foundation that got me where I am today, writing this book. Sharvari, thank you for always being my biggest cheerleader and for standing by me through every high and low. You've taught me something truly priceless – that relationships matter more than any amount of money ever could. You also showed me that there's no other path to success but via discipline. And that, I realize, is also the most important ingredient in sound money management. Aarohi and Aariv, your smiles are my daily reminder to stay mindful and responsible with our money and our future. You give my life purpose and shape the way I think about everything – especially money. This book is as much yours as it is ours.